HTML5 AND CSS3 ESSENTIALS

Design Responsive, Accessible Websites for the Modern Web

THOMPSON CARTER

TABLE OF CONTENTS

INTRODUCTION..6

CHAPTER 1: THE EVOLUTION OF HTML AND CSS...............12

CHAPTER 2: SETTING UP YOUR DEVELOPMENT
ENVIRONMENT 19

CHAPTER 3: THE BUILDING BLOCKS OF A WEBSITE 27

CHAPTER 4: HTML5 SYNTAX AND SEMANTICS....................37

CHAPTER 5: WORKING WITH TEXT AND MULTIMEDIA
CONTENT...46

CHAPTER 6: CREATING LINKS AND NAVIGATION...............55

CHAPTER 7: HTML5 FORMS AND USER INPUT 64

CHAPTER 8: ADVANCED HTML5 FEATURES 73

CHAPTER 9: INTRODUCTION TO CSS3 82

CHAPTER 10: WORKING WITH COLORS, FONTS, AND
TYPOGRAPHY 92

CHAPTER 11: LAYOUT BASICS WITH CSS3 101

CHAPTER 12: MODERN LAYOUTS WITH FLEXBOX 110

CHAPTER 13: ADVANCED LAYOUTS WITH CSS GRID 121

CHAPTER 14: RESPONSIVE DESIGN WITH MEDIA QUERIES 130

CHAPTER 15: CSS3 TRANSITIONS AND ANIMATIONS..........139

CHAPTER 16: PSEUDO-CLASSES AND PSEUDO-ELEMENTS 149

CHAPTER 17: WORKING WITH CSS VARIABLES 159

CHAPTER 18: INTRODUCTION TO JAVASCRIPT FOR HTML5 AND CSS3 168

CHAPTER 19: WEB ACCESSIBILITY (A11Y) BASICS.................178

CHAPTER 20: OPTIMIZING PERFORMANCE 185

CHAPTER 21: CROSS-BROWSER COMPATIBILITY 193

CHAPTER 22: DEPLOYING YOUR WEBSITE...........................201

CHAPTER 23: BUILDING A PORTFOLIO WEBSITE...............210

CHAPTER 24: CREATING A BLOG LAYOUT 218

CHAPTER 25: DESIGNING AN E-COMMERCE LANDING PAGE..227

Introduction

In today's digital era, web development has become a vital skill for creating interactive, accessible, and visually appealing websites. From personal portfolios to powerful e-commerce platforms, the demand for well-designed and high-performing websites has skyrocketed. **HTML5 and CSS3 Essentials: Design Responsive, Accessible Websites for the Modern Web** is your comprehensive guide to mastering these foundational technologies and crafting professional websites that stand out.

Why This Book?

The internet is ever-evolving, with new standards, tools, and practices continually emerging. As a beginner or an aspiring web developer, navigating this dynamic landscape can feel overwhelming. This book is designed to demystify web development by breaking it down into digestible steps, teaching you the core principles of **HTML5** and **CSS3**, and equipping you with the skills to build real-world projects. Whether you're a novice with no prior coding experience or someone looking to refine their skills, this book provides a structured, jargon-free approach that empowers you to create responsive, accessible, and visually engaging websites.

What You Will Learn

This book is divided into six comprehensive parts, each focusing on a specific aspect of web development, to ensure you build a strong foundation while progressively tackling more advanced concepts.

1. **Getting Started with Web Development:** Understand the history and evolution of HTML and CSS, set up your development environment, and explore the essential building blocks of modern web design.

2. **Mastering HTML5:** Learn how to structure your content using semantic elements, work with forms, integrate multimedia, and leverage advanced features like <canvas> and <svg> for interactive graphics.

3. **Mastering CSS3:** Dive into the art of styling your website. From working with colors, fonts, and layouts to mastering Flexbox, Grid, and animations, this section equips you with the tools to create visually stunning designs.

4. **Interactivity with JavaScript:** Discover how JavaScript enhances your HTML5 and CSS3 projects by adding interactivity, such as dropdown menus, modals, and dynamic animations. You'll also learn to integrate popular JavaScript libraries to simplify complex tasks.

7

5. **Accessibility, Optimization, and Deployment:** Create inclusive websites by following accessibility best practices, optimize performance for faster load times, and deploy your projects to make them live on the web.

6. **Real-World Projects:** Apply your knowledge by building professional-grade projects, including a portfolio website, a blog platform, and an e-commerce landing page, while focusing on responsive design, SEO, and usability.

Key Features of This Book

- **Jargon-Free Explanations:** Complex concepts are broken down into simple, easy-to-understand terms, ensuring clarity and accessibility for readers of all levels.

- **Real-World Examples:** Learn by doing with hands-on examples that simulate real-world scenarios. Each chapter includes practical exercises to reinforce your understanding.

- **Step-by-Step Guidance:** Follow a structured approach to building projects, with clear instructions and code snippets for every step.

- **Focus on Best Practices:** Gain insights into modern web design principles, including responsive design, accessibility standards, and performance optimization.
- **Interactive Learning:** Incorporate animations, interactivity, and advanced layouts into your projects to create dynamic user experiences.

Who Is This Book For?

This book is designed for:

- **Beginners:** Individuals who want to start their journey in web development and need a reliable, step-by-step guide.
- **Aspiring Designers:** Creative professionals looking to enhance their skills by learning how to structure and style websites effectively.
- **Career Switchers:** Those transitioning into tech and seeking to master web development fundamentals.
- **Students and Educators:** Learners seeking a practical resource for project-based study.

No prior experience in coding is necessary—just curiosity, determination, and a desire to learn!

How to Use This Book

Each chapter builds on the knowledge from the previous one, so it's best to progress sequentially. As you work through the chapters, you'll:

- Write, test, and debug code using your chosen tools.
- Build hands-on projects that reinforce theoretical concepts.
- Experiment with code examples to deepen your understanding.

To get the most out of this book:

1. Set up your development environment as described in the first chapter.
2. Practice regularly by completing exercises and experimenting with the code.
3. Challenge yourself with the real-world projects in the final section.

The Journey Ahead

By the end of this book, you'll have the skills to design, develop, and deploy professional websites that are responsive, accessible, and optimized for modern web standards. You'll not only understand the technologies behind the web but also gain the confidence to bring your ideas to life.

So, whether you're dreaming of building your first portfolio, creating an engaging blog, or launching a sleek e-commerce platform, this book is your gateway to the exciting world of web development. Let's embark on this journey together—one line of code at a time.

Chapter 1: The Evolution of HTML and CSS

---

1. Brief History of HTML and CSS

The Origins of HTML:

- **HTML (HyperText Markup Language)** was created by Tim Berners-Lee in 1991 as a simple language for sharing documents on the World Wide Web.
- The initial version of HTML focused on basic text formatting, hyperlinks, and images.
- Over time, HTML evolved to include more sophisticated features like tables, forms, and multimedia support.

The Evolution of HTML Versions:

- **HTML 2.0 (1995):** Introduced standards for the web, including forms and tables.
- **HTML 3.2 (1997):** Added support for scripting languages like JavaScript and styling with CSS.
- **HTML 4.01 (1999):** Focused on separating content (HTML) from presentation (CSS).
- **XHTML (2000):** A stricter version of HTML that followed XML syntax rules.

- **HTML5 (2014):** The latest standard, designed for modern web applications, introduced semantic elements, multimedia support, and APIs.

The Birth of CSS:

- **CSS (Cascading Style Sheets)** was introduced by Håkon Wium Lie in 1996 to separate the content of a webpage (HTML) from its design and layout.
- Before CSS, all styling had to be embedded directly in HTML, leading to cluttered and hard-to-maintain code.

---

2. The Shift to HTML5 and CSS3
Why HTML5 and CSS3?

- As web technology advanced, the need for a language that supported modern demands like multimedia, responsive design, and interactivity became clear.
- **HTML5** and **CSS3** addressed these needs:
  - HTML5 introduced semantic elements, multimedia support without plugins (e.g., <audio> and <video>), and APIs like Web Storage and Geolocation.
  - CSS3 brought advanced styling capabilities like gradients, animations, transitions, and media queries.

Key Improvements in HTML5:

1. **Semantic Elements:**
   - o Introduced elements like \<header>, \<footer>, \<section>, and \<article> to structure content logically.
   - o Improves SEO and accessibility by helping browsers and screen readers understand content better.

2. **Built-in Multimedia Support:**
   - o Added native tags for video (\<video>) and audio (\<audio>), eliminating the need for plugins like Flash.

3. **APIs for Modern Applications:**
   - o Web Storage API for local data storage (localStorage and sessionStorage).
   - o Geolocation API for location-based services.
   - o Canvas and SVG for graphics.

Key Improvements in CSS3:

1. **Advanced Styling:**
   - o Gradient backgrounds, shadows, and rounded corners without images.
   - o New color formats like RGBA and HSL.

2. **Responsive Design:**

  o Media queries allow developers to create designs that adapt to different screen sizes.

3. **Transitions and Animations:**
  o Smooth animations using only CSS, enhancing user experience without JavaScript.

4. **Grid and Flexbox Layouts:**
  o Modern tools for creating flexible, responsive layouts with minimal code.

---

3. Why HTML5 and CSS3 Are Essential for Modern Web Development

1. Enhanced User Experience:

- Semantic HTML improves the structure and readability of webpages for both users and search engines.
- CSS3 allows for visually appealing designs with animations and interactive elements.

2. Mobile-First Development:

- HTML5 and CSS3 support responsive design, enabling websites to work seamlessly on various devices and screen sizes.

3. Accessibility:

- HTML5 introduces accessibility features like ARIA roles and attributes to ensure that websites are usable for people with disabilities.

4. Speed and Performance:

- CSS3's ability to replace images for visual effects (e.g., gradients, shadows) reduces load times.
- HTML5 APIs like Web Storage eliminate the need for server-side storage for small datasets.

5. Future-Proofing:

- HTML5 and CSS3 are supported by all modern browsers, ensuring compatibility and longevity for web applications.

---

4. Overview of Responsive and Accessible Design Principles

Responsive Design Principles:

1. **Fluid Layouts:** Use relative units (%, em, rem) instead of fixed units (px) for widths and font sizes.
2. **Media Queries:** Adapt styles based on the device's screen size.
   - Example:

     css

```css
@media (max-width: 768px) {
  body {
    font-size: 14px;
  }
}
```

3. **Flexible Images:** Ensure images resize dynamically within their containers.

   o Example:

   css

```css
img {
  max-width: 100%;
  height: auto;
}
```

Accessible Design Principles:

1. **Keyboard Navigation:** Ensure all interactive elements can be navigated using a keyboard.
2. **Semantic HTML:** Use proper HTML tags (e.g., <button> for buttons) to help screen readers interpret content.
3. **ARIA Roles:** Use ARIA attributes like aria-label to provide additional context.
4. **Contrast and Legibility:** Maintain sufficient contrast between text and background colors.

The evolution of HTML and CSS has been a journey toward creating a more structured, visually appealing, and user-friendly web. With HTML5 and CSS3, developers can design websites that are not only beautiful but also functional, accessible, and responsive. Mastering these technologies is essential for any modern web developer, and this chapter has set the foundation for deeper exploration in the upcoming sections. Let's dive into the details of HTML5 in the next chapter!

Chapter 2: Setting Up Your Development Environment

1. Tools for Web Development

To develop modern, responsive websites, you need a set of essential tools to streamline your workflow. These tools fall into the following categories:

1. Code Editors:

- Code editors are where you write and manage your HTML, CSS, and JavaScript files. The best editors offer features like syntax highlighting, autocomplete, and debugging tools.
    - **Visual Studio Code (VS Code):** A free, powerful editor with extensive extensions and debugging capabilities.
    - **Sublime Text:** Lightweight and fast, with a rich ecosystem of plugins.
    - **Atom:** An open-source editor created by GitHub, known for its flexibility.

2. Web Browsers:

- Browsers render your HTML and CSS code and allow you to test your websites.
    - **Google Chrome:** Known for its robust developer tools.
    - **Mozilla Firefox:** Offers excellent debugging tools and a focus on privacy.
    - **Microsoft Edge:** Built on Chromium, compatible with Chrome extensions.
    - **Safari:** Useful for testing websites on macOS and iOS.

---

3. Version Control:

- Version control systems help track changes in your code and collaborate with others.
    - **Git:** The most widely used version control system.
    - **GitHub:** A platform for hosting and sharing your Git repositories.
    - **Git GUI Clients:** Tools like GitHub Desktop and Sourcetree provide a graphical interface for Git.

---

2. Installing and Using Code Editors

Here's how to set up the most popular code editors:

1. Visual Studio Code (VS Code):

- **Installation:**
  - Download from https://code.visualstudio.com/.
  - Install for your operating system (Windows, macOS, or Linux).

- **Features:**
  - Extensions for web development, like Live Server, Prettier, and Emmet.
  - Built-in Git support.

- **Getting Started:**

  0. Open VS Code.
  1. Create a new file and save it as index.html.
  2. Install the "Live Server" extension to preview changes in real-time.
  3. Use shortcuts like Ctrl + / (comment/uncomment code) and Ctrl + Shift + P (command palette).

---

2. Sublime Text:

- **Installation:**
  - Download from https://www.sublimetext.com/.
- **Features:**
  - Fast startup and minimal memory usage.

    o Supports packages like Emmet for HTML and CSS shortcuts.

- **Getting Started:**

0. Open Sublime Text.
1. Create a new file and save it as index.html.
2. Install Package Control to add plugins for syntax highlighting and code linting.

---

3. Atom:

- **Installation:**
  - o Download from https://atom.io/.
- **Features:**
  - o Built-in Git and GitHub integration.
  - o Highly customizable with themes and plugins.
- **Getting Started:**

0. Open Atom.
1. Create a new file and save it as index.html.
2. Use the Teletype plugin for real-time collaboration.

---

3. Understanding Browser Developer Tools

Every modern browser comes equipped with developer tools (DevTools) that are essential for web development.

1. Accessing DevTools:

- Open a webpage and press F12 or Ctrl + Shift + I (Windows) / Cmd + Option + I (Mac).

2. Key Features:

- **Elements Tab:** Inspect and edit HTML and CSS in real-time.
- **Console Tab:** Test JavaScript code and view error messages.
- **Network Tab:** Analyze network requests and responses.
- **Performance Tab:** Measure website loading and rendering performance.

Example: Inspecting and Editing HTML/CSS

1. Right-click an element on the webpage and select "Inspect."
2. Modify the HTML or CSS directly in the Elements tab and see changes in real-time.

4. Basics of HTML and CSS File Structures

A well-organized file structure is critical for managing web projects efficiently.

1. File Naming and Organization:

- Use lowercase letters for file and folder names.
- Keep file names descriptive (e.g., style.css or about.html).
- Structure your project logically:

perl

```
my-website/
├── index.html
├── styles/
│   └── style.css
├── scripts/
│   └── script.js
├── images/
│   └── logo.png
```

2. HTML File Basics:

- Save HTML files with the .html extension.
- Basic structure of an HTML file:

html

```
<!DOCTYPE html>
<html lang="en">
<head>
  <meta charset="UTF-8">
  <meta name="viewport" content="width=device-width, initial-scale=1.0">
  <title>My First Website</title>
```

```html
    <link rel="stylesheet" href="styles/style.css">
  </head>
  <body>
    <h1>Welcome to My Website</h1>
    <p>This is a paragraph of text.</p>
  </body>
</html>
```

3. CSS File Basics:

- Save CSS files with the .css extension.
- Example of a simple CSS file:

css

```css
body {
    font-family: Arial, sans-serif;
    background-color: #f4f4f4;
    margin: 0;
    padding: 0;
}

h1 {
    color: #333;
    text-align: center;
}

p {
    color: #666;
    line-height: 1.5;
}
```

4. Linking HTML and CSS:

- Use the <link> tag in the <head> section of your HTML file:

html

```
<link rel="stylesheet" href="styles/style.css">
```

A well-equipped development environment sets the stage for efficient and effective web design. With a reliable code editor, a solid understanding of browser developer tools, and a clean project structure, you're ready to start building and experimenting with HTML and CSS. In the next chapter, we'll dive into the foundational elements of an HTML5 document and explore the syntax and semantics that make up the web. Let's get coding!

Chapter 3: The Building Blocks of a Website

---

1. What Are HTML and CSS, and How Do They Work Together?
HTML (HyperText Markup Language):

- HTML is the standard language for creating the structure and content of a webpage.
- It defines elements like headings, paragraphs, images, links, and forms using tags.

CSS (Cascading Style Sheets):

- CSS is used to style and format HTML content.
- It controls visual aspects like colors, fonts, layouts, and animations.

How They Work Together:

- HTML provides the **skeleton** of the webpage, and CSS adds the **skin** to make it visually appealing.
- Example:

html

```
<!DOCTYPE html>
```

```
<html lang="en">
<head>
  <title>Example Page</title>
  <link rel="stylesheet" href="style.css">
</head>
<body>
  <h1>Welcome to My Website</h1>
  <p>This is a sample paragraph.</p>
</body>
</html>
css
```

```
/* style.css */
h1 {
   color: blue;
   text-align: center;
}


p {
   font-size: 16px;
   color: gray;
}
```

2. Introduction to the DOM (Document Object Model)

What Is the DOM?

- The Document Object Model (DOM) is a programming interface for web documents.

- It represents the structure of an HTML document as a tree of nodes.
- Each element in the HTML file (e.g., <h1>, <p>) becomes a node in the DOM.

Why Is the DOM Important?

- The DOM allows JavaScript and other scripts to interact with and manipulate the webpage dynamically.
- Example: Changing the text of a heading using JavaScript:

html

```
<h1 id="title">Original Title</h1>
<script>
   document.getElementById("title").textContent = "Updated Title";
</script>
```

DOM Tree Example: For this HTML:

html

```
<!DOCTYPE html>
<html>
<head>
  <title>DOM Example</title>
</head>
<body>
  <h1>Welcome</h1>
  <p>This is an example paragraph.</p>
```

```
</body>
</html>
```

The DOM tree structure:

less

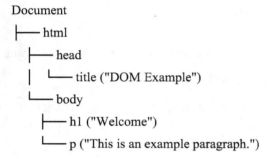

```
Document
├── html
    ├── head
    │   └── title ("DOM Example")
    └── body
        ├── h1 ("Welcome")
        └── p ("This is an example paragraph.")
```

---

3. Anatomy of an HTML Document

Every HTML document follows a standard structure:

1. **Doctype Declaration:**
    o   Tells the browser to render the document using HTML5 standards.
    o   Example:

        html

        <!DOCTYPE html>

2. **HTML Element:**
    o   The root element enclosing all other elements.
    o   Example:

html

```
<html lang="en">
</html>
```

3. **Head Section:**

    o Contains metadata about the document (e.g., title, character encoding, styles).

    o Example:

html

```
<head>
    <title>Page Title</title>
    <meta charset="UTF-8">
</head>
```

4. **Body Section:**

    o Contains the visible content of the webpage (e.g., text, images, videos).

    o Example:

html

```
<body>
    <h1>Welcome to My Page</h1>
    <p>This is the body content.</p>
</body>
```

Complete Example:

html

```
<!DOCTYPE html>
<html lang="en">
<head>
  <meta charset="UTF-8">
  <meta name="viewport" content="width=device-width, initial-scale=1.0">
  <title>Basic HTML Document</title>
</head>
<body>
  <h1>Hello, World!</h1>
  <p>This is a basic HTML document.</p>
</body>
</html>
```

4. Linking CSS to HTML Files

CSS can be applied to an HTML document in three ways:

1. **Inline CSS:**
   - Applied directly to an HTML element using the style attribute.
   - Example:

     html

     ```
     <h1 style="color: red;">Inline Styled Heading</h1>
     ```

2. **Internal CSS:**
   - Written within a <style> tag in the <head> section.

o Example:

html

```
<head>
  <style>
    h1 {
      color: blue;
    }
  </style>
</head>
```

3. **External CSS:**
   o Written in a separate file and linked to the HTML using a <link> tag.
   o Example:

html

```
<head>
  <link rel="stylesheet" href="styles.css">
</head>
```

   o Example CSS file (styles.css):

css

```
body {
  font-family: Arial, sans-serif;
}
```

```
h1 {
    color: green;
}
```

Best Practice: Use external CSS for maintainability and scalability.

---

5. Best Practices for Structuring Your Code

1. Use Semantic HTML:

- Write meaningful HTML by using tags like <header>, <footer>, <article>, and <section>.
- Example:

html

```
<header>
    <h1>Website Title</h1>
</header>
<section>
    <p>Main content goes here.</p>
</section>
<footer>
    <p>&copy; 2025 My Website</p>
</footer>
```

2. Indent Your Code:

- Use consistent indentation (2 or 4 spaces) for better readability.

3. Organize Your Files:

- Use a logical folder structure:

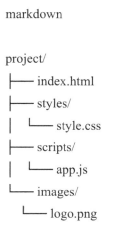

```
project/
├── index.html
├── styles/
│   └── style.css
├── scripts/
│   └── app.js
└── images/
    └── logo.png
```

4. Comment Your Code:

- Add comments to explain complex sections of code.
- Example:

html

```html
<!-- This is the main heading -->
<h1>Welcome</h1>
```

5. Use Meaningful Class and ID Names:

- Avoid generic names like div1 or style2.
- Example:

html

```
<div id="main-content" class="featured">
  <p>Important content goes here.</p>
</div>
```

6. Validate Your HTML and CSS:

- Use online validators like <u>W3C Validator</u> to ensure your code is standards-compliant.

HTML and CSS are the backbone of web design, working together to create the structure and style of a website. Understanding the DOM, the anatomy of an HTML document, and best practices for linking and organizing code lays a strong foundation for efficient and professional web development. In the next chapter, we'll dive deeper into the essential syntax and semantics of HTML5 to create meaningful and accessible web content. Let's build!

Chapter 4: HTML5 Syntax and Semantics

---

1. Basic Structure and Elements of an HTML5 Document

An HTML5 document is a blueprint that defines the content and structure of a webpage. It provides the foundation upon which all styles and functionality are built.

HTML5 Document Structure:

1. **Doctype Declaration:**
   - Specifies the version of HTML being used.
   - Declares the document as HTML5:

   html

   ```
   <!DOCTYPE html>
   ```

2. **HTML Element:**
   - Wraps the entire document.
   - Contains two primary sections: <head> and <body>.

   html

   ```
   <html lang="en">
     <head>...</head>
   ```

```
<body>...</body>
</html>
```

3. **Head Section:**

   o Contains metadata and links to resources like CSS and JavaScript files.

   o Common elements include:

     ▪ <title>: Sets the page title (displayed on the browser tab).

     ▪ <meta>: Provides information like character encoding and viewport settings.

     ▪ <link>: Links external stylesheets.

     ▪ <script>: Links external JavaScript files.

4. **Body Section:**

   o Contains the visible content of the page (text, images, links, forms, etc.).

Complete HTML5 Example:

html

```
<!DOCTYPE html>
<html lang="en">
<head>
  <meta charset="UTF-8">
  <meta name="viewport" content="width=device-width, initial-scale=1.0">
  <meta name="description" content="Learn HTML5 Syntax and Semantics">
  <title>HTML5 Basics</title>
```

```
<link rel="stylesheet" href="styles.css">
</head>
<body>
  <header>
    <h1>Welcome to HTML5</h1>
  </header>
  <main>
    <section>
      <p>HTML5 provides structure and meaning to web content.</p>
    </section>
  </main>
  <footer>
    <p>&copy; 2025 Web Development</p>
  </footer>
</body>
</html>
```

2. HTML5 Doctype Declaration

The <!DOCTYPE> declaration in HTML5:

- Informs the browser to render the document in standards mode.
- Simplified compared to previous versions (e.g., XHTML):

  html

  <!DOCTYPE html>

Why Is the Doctype Important?

- Prevents browsers from falling back to quirks mode (an outdated rendering mode used for legacy web pages).
- Ensures consistent rendering across modern browsers.

---

3. *The Role of Semantic Elements*
What Are Semantic Elements?

- Semantic elements convey meaning about their content to both browsers and developers.
- Examples include <header>, <nav>, <main>, <section>, <article>, <footer>, and <aside>.

Why Are They Important?

- Improve code readability and maintainability.
- Help search engines and assistive technologies understand the structure of the page.

Key Semantic Elements:

1. **<header>:**
   - Represents the introductory content or navigation links.
   - Typically appears at the top of a page or section.
   - Example:

html

```
<header>
  <h1>My Website</h1>
  <nav>
    <ul>
      <li><a href="#home">Home</a></li>
      <li><a href="#about">About</a></li>
    </ul>
  </nav>
</header>
```

2. **<nav>:**

- o Defines a block of navigation links.
- o Example:

html

```
<nav>
  <ul>
    <li><a href="#services">Services</a></li>
    <li><a href="#contact">Contact</a></li>
  </ul>
</nav>
```

3. **<main>:**

- o Represents the main content of a document.
- o Should not include repeated content like headers, footers, or sidebars.

o Example:

html

```
<main>
  <h2>About Us</h2>
  <p>We are a web development company.</p>
</main>
```

4. **<section>:**

o Groups related content within a document.

o Often used with headings.

o Example:

html

```
<section>
  <h2>Our Services</h2>
  <p>We provide web design and development services.</p>
</section>
```

5. **<article>:**

o Represents independent content that could stand alone (e.g., blog posts, news articles).

o Example:

html

```
<article>
```

```
<h2>Latest Blog Post</h2>
<p>Discover the benefits of HTML5 and CSS3.</p>
</article>
```

6. **<footer>**:

   o Contains information about its parent section or the entire document.

   o Example:

   html

```
<footer>
    <p>Contact us at info@example.com</p>
</footer>
```

7. **<aside>**:

   o Represents complementary content, such as sidebars or callout boxes.

   o Example:

   html

```
<aside>
    <p>Related articles: <a href="#html5">Understanding HTML5</a></p>
</aside>
```

4. Benefits of Semantic HTML for SEO and Accessibility

1. For SEO (Search Engine Optimization):

- Semantic elements help search engines understand the content hierarchy and structure.
- Improved content indexing leads to better search rankings.
- Example: <article> elements are prioritized in search results as standalone content.

2. For Accessibility:

- Assistive technologies (e.g., screen readers) use semantic elements to navigate web content.
- Semantic tags reduce confusion for users relying on these tools.
- Example:
  - <nav> signals a navigation area, allowing screen readers to skip directly to it.

3. For Code Readability and Maintenance:

- Semantic elements make code easier to read and understand for developers.
- Facilitates teamwork and debugging.

4. For Consistency Across Browsers:

- Modern browsers have built-in support for semantic HTML, ensuring consistent behavior.

HTML5 introduces a cleaner, more meaningful way to structure web pages through semantic elements. These elements enhance user experience, improve search engine rankings, and make websites more accessible. By understanding and implementing the syntax and semantics of HTML5, you lay the foundation for building modern, professional web applications. In the next chapter, we'll dive deeper into working with multimedia and text content in HTML5. Let's keep building!

Chapter 5: Working with Text and Multimedia Content

---

1. Text Elements

Text is the foundation of any webpage, and HTML5 offers a variety of elements to structure and present text effectively.

1.1 Headings:

- Headings (<h1> to <h6>) define the structure and hierarchy of your content.
- <h1> is the highest-level heading (used for main titles), while <h6> is the lowest.
- Example:

html

```
<h1>Main Title</h1>
<h2>Subheading</h2>
<h3>Sub-subheading</h3>
```

Best Practices:

- Use only one <h1> per page for SEO.

- Maintain a logical order of headings (e.g., <h1> followed by <h2>).

1.2 Paragraphs:

- Use the <p> element to structure text into readable blocks.
- Example:

html

<p>This is a paragraph of text on a webpage. It provides detailed information about the topic at hand.</p>

1.3 Lists:

- HTML supports two types of lists:
  - **Ordered Lists (<ol>):** Automatically numbered.

    html

    ```
    <ol>
       <li>Step 1</li>
       <li>Step 2</li>
       <li>Step 3</li>
    </ol>
    ```

  - **Unordered Lists (<ul>):** Bulleted lists.

html

```
<ul>
  <li>Item 1</li>
  <li>Item 2</li>
  <li>Item 3</li>
</ul>
```

Nested Lists:

- Create sublists by nesting <ul> or <ol> inside <li> elements.

html

```
<ul>
  <li>Main Item
    <ul>
      <li>Sub Item 1</li>
      <li>Sub Item 2</li>
    </ul>
  </li>
</ul>
```

1.4 Blockquotes:

- Use <blockquote> for long quotations.
- Example:

html

```
<blockquote cite="https://example.com">
    This is a blockquote that highlights a large section of quoted text.
</blockquote>
```

2. Adding and Formatting Images in HTML5

Images play a crucial role in web design, and HTML5 makes adding and formatting them straightforward.

2.1 Basic Image Tag:

- Use the <img> tag to add images.
- Attributes:
  - src: Path to the image.
  - alt: Alternative text for accessibility.
- Example:

html

```
<img src="images/photo.jpg" alt="A beautiful landscape">
```

2.2 Common Attributes:

- width and height: Set image dimensions.

html

```
<img    src="images/photo.jpg"    alt="Landscape"    width="300"
height="200">
```

- title: Adds a tooltip when hovered over.

html

```
<img   src="images/photo.jpg"   alt="Landscape"   title="A   beautiful
landscape">
```

2.3 Responsive Images:

- Use max-width in CSS to ensure images adapt to screen sizes.

css

```
img {
    max-width: 100%;
    height: auto;
}
```

3. Embedding Videos and Audio

HTML5 provides native support for multimedia elements without requiring plugins like Flash.

3.1 Adding Videos:

- Use the <video> tag to embed videos.
- Attributes:
    - controls: Adds play, pause, and volume controls.
    - autoplay: Automatically plays the video.
    - loop: Replays the video continuously.
- Example:

html

```
<video src="videos/sample.mp4" controls width="640" height="360">
    Your browser does not support the video tag.
</video>
```

Adding Multiple Formats:

- Use <source> to provide different video formats for browser compatibility.

html

```
<video controls>
    <source src="videos/sample.mp4" type="video/mp4">
    <source src="videos/sample.webm" type="video/webm">
    Your browser does not support the video tag.
</video>
```

3.2 Adding Audio:

- Use the <audio> tag to embed audio.

- Attributes:
    - controls: Adds play, pause, and volume controls.
    - autoplay: Automatically plays the audio.
    - loop: Replays the audio continuously.
- Example:

html

```
<audio src="audio/song.mp3" controls>
    Your browser does not support the audio tag.
</audio>
```

Adding Multiple Formats:

- Use <source> for compatibility with different audio formats.

html

```
<audio controls>
    <source src="audio/song.mp3" type="audio/mpeg">
    <source src="audio/song.ogg" type="audio/ogg">
    Your browser does not support the audio tag.
</audio>
```

---

4. Using the <picture> and <source> Elements for Responsive Media

The <picture> element allows you to serve different image files based on device or browser capabilities.

4.1 Responsive Images with <picture>:

- Use <source> inside <picture> to define multiple image options.
- Example:

html

```
<picture>
    <source srcset="images/large.jpg" media="(min-width: 768px)">
    <source srcset="images/small.jpg" media="(max-width: 767px)">
    <img src="images/default.jpg" alt="A responsive image">
</picture>
```

How It Works:

- srcset specifies different image files.
- media sets the condition (e.g., screen width) for each image.

4.2 Using <source> for Video Optimization:

- Provide multiple video formats for different browsers.
- Example:

html

```
<video controls>
    <source src="videos/sample.mp4" type="video/mp4">
    <source src="videos/sample.webm" type="video/webm">
    Your browser does not support the video tag.
```

    </video>

HTML5's robust support for text and multimedia content allows developers to create engaging and accessible web pages. By mastering text elements, formatting images, embedding audio and video, and using responsive media techniques like <picture> and <source>, you can enhance the visual and functional quality of your websites. In the next chapter, we'll explore creating and styling navigation links and menus to improve user experience. Let's continue building!

Chapter 6: Creating Links and Navigation

1. Adding Internal, External, and Anchor Links

Links are the core of the web, enabling navigation between pages, sections, and external resources. HTML5 provides a flexible and powerful way to create links with the <a> (anchor) element.

1.1 Internal Links:

- Used to navigate between pages within the same website.
- Example:

html

```
<a href="about.html">About Us</a>
<a href="contact.html">Contact</a>
```

1.2 External Links:

- Used to navigate to other websites.
- Example:

html

```
<a href="https://www.example.com" target="_blank" rel="noopener
noreferrer">Visit Example</a>
```

- **Attributes:**
  - target="_blank": Opens the link in a new tab.
  - rel="noopener noreferrer": Improves security by preventing the new page from accessing the linking page's window object.

1.3 Anchor Links (In-Page Navigation):

- Used to navigate to specific sections within the same page.
- Requires the id attribute for the target element.
- Example:

html

```
<!-- Navigation Link -->
<a href="#section1">Go to Section 1</a>

<!-- Target Section -->
<h2 id="section1">Section 1</h2>
<p>This is the content of Section 1.</p>
```

1.4 Email and Telephone Links:

- Email Link:

  html

  <a href="mailto:example@example.com">Send an Email</a>

- Telephone Link:

  html

  <a href="tel:+1234567890">Call Us</a>

---

2. Best Practices for Navigation Menus

A well-structured navigation menu is essential for enhancing user experience and accessibility. Follow these best practices:

2.1 Use Unordered Lists for Menus:

- Wrap navigation links in a <ul> to create a logical structure.
- Example:

  html

  ```
  <ul>
     <li><a href="index.html">Home</a></li>
     <li><a href="services.html">Services</a></li>
     <li><a href="contact.html">Contact</a></li>
  </ul>
  ```

2.2 Highlight the Current Page:

- Use a class like active to indicate the active page in the navigation.
- Example:

html

```
<ul>
    <li><a href="index.html" class="active">Home</a></li>
    <li><a href="services.html">Services</a></li>
    <li><a href="contact.html">Contact</a></li>
</ul>
```

- CSS for the active link:

css

```
.active {
    font-weight: bold;
    color: #007BFF;
}
```

2.3 Keep It Simple:

- Limit the number of menu items to avoid overwhelming users.

- Use drop-down menus for sub-navigation.

2.4 Ensure Responsiveness:

- Use CSS media queries to create responsive navigation menus.
- Example:

```css
css

@media (max-width: 768px) {
  nav ul {
    display: flex;
    flex-direction: column;
  }
}
```

3. Using <nav> for Semantic Navigation
What Is the <nav> Element?

- The <nav> element is a semantic container for primary navigation links.
- It helps browsers, search engines, and assistive technologies understand the navigation structure.

Example of a Semantic Navigation Menu:

html

```
<nav>
  <ul>
    <li><a href="index.html">Home</a></li>
    <li><a href="about.html">About</a></li>
    <li><a href="services.html">Services</a></li>
    <li><a href="contact.html">Contact</a></li>
  </ul>
</nav>
```

When to Use <nav>:

- Use <nav> for primary navigation links (e.g., main menu, footer menu).
- Do not use <nav> for unrelated groups of links (e.g., inline links in an article).

---

4. Accessibility Considerations for Navigation

Accessible navigation ensures that all users, including those with disabilities, can easily navigate your website.

4.1 Use Descriptive Link Text:

- Avoid generic phrases like "Click Here."
- Example:

html

<a href="services.html">View Our Services</a>

4.2 Provide Keyboard Navigation:

- Ensure all navigation links can be accessed via the Tab key.

4.3 Use ARIA Landmarks:

- Add aria-label to the <nav> element for screen readers.
- Example:

html

```
<nav aria-label="Main Navigation">
  <ul>
    <li><a href="home.html">Home</a></li>
    <li><a href="about.html">About Us</a></li>
  </ul>
</nav>
```

4.4 Skip Links:

- Add a "Skip to Content" link for users to bypass repetitive navigation.
- Example:

html

```html
<a href="#main-content" class="skip-link">Skip to Content</a>
<main id="main-content">
   <h1>Welcome to Our Website</h1>
</main>
```

- CSS for Skip Link Visibility:

css

```css
.skip-link {
   position: absolute;
   top: -40px;
   left: 0;
   background: #007BFF;
   color: #fff;
   padding: 8px;
   z-index: 100;
}

.skip-link:focus {
   top: 0;
}
```

Navigation is the backbone of any website's usability and structure. By mastering internal, external, and anchor links, adhering to best practices for menus, leveraging the semantic <nav> element, and implementing accessibility features, you can create an intuitive and inclusive navigation system. In the next chapter, we'll explore how to build and style forms using HTML5 to gather user input effectively. Let's keep creating!

Chapter 7: HTML5 Forms and User Input

---

1. Building Forms with <form>, <input>, <textarea>, and <select>

Forms are essential for collecting user input on the web, from contact details to preferences. HTML5 provides a variety of elements to create robust and user-friendly forms.

1.1 The <form> Element:

- The <form> element acts as a container for all form controls.
- Attributes:
    - action: Specifies where to send form data.
    - method: Specifies how to send the form data (GET or POST).
- Example:

html

```
<form action="/submit" method="POST">
    <!-- Form controls go here -->
</form>
```

1.2 The <input> Element:

- The <input> element is used for various types of user input.
- Common types of <input>:
  - o text: For single-line text input.
  - o email: For email addresses.
  - o password: Masks the input for sensitive data.
  - o number: For numeric values.
  - o checkbox and radio: For selecting options.
  - o submit: A button to submit the form.
- Example:

html

```html
<form action="/submit" method="POST">
    <label for="name">Name:</label>
    <input type="text" id="name" name="name" required>

    <label for="email">Email:</label>
    <input type="email" id="email" name="email" required>

    <button type="submit">Submit</button>
</form>
```

1.3 The <textarea> Element:

- Used for multi-line text input.
- Example:

html

```
<label for="message">Message:</label>
<textarea id="message" name="message" rows="4"
cols="50"></textarea>
```

1.4 The <select> Element:

- Creates a dropdown menu.
- Example:

html

```
<label for="country">Choose your country:</label>
<select id="country" name="country">
   <option value="us">United States</option>
   <option value="uk">United Kingdom</option>
   <option value="ca">Canada</option>
</select>
```

2. HTML5 Form Validation Attributes

HTML5 introduces built-in validation attributes to improve form reliability and user experience.

2.1 Required Fields:

- Ensures the field is filled before submitting.
- Example:

html

```
<input type="text" name="username" required>
```

2.2 Pattern Matching:

- Validates input against a regular expression.
- Example: Validate a phone number format:

html

```
<input type="text" name="phone" pattern="[0-9]{3}-[0-9]{3}-[0-9]{4}" title="Format: 123-456-7890">
```

2.3 Email Validation:

- Ensures the input is a valid email address.
- Example:

html

```
<input type="email" name="email" required>
```

2.4 Number Ranges:

- Restricts numeric input to a specific range.
- Example:

html

```
<input type="number" name="age" min="18" max="99">
```

2.5 Placeholder Text:

- Displays a hint inside the input field.
- Example:

html

```
<input type="text" name="username" placeholder="Enter your username">
```

3. Creating Accessible Forms Using Labels and Fieldsets

Accessibility ensures that forms are usable by everyone, including people with disabilities.

3.1 Labels:

- Labels describe the purpose of form controls and should be explicitly associated with them using the for attribute.
- Example:

html

```
<label for="email">Email Address:</label>
<input type="email" id="email" name="email" required>
```

3.2 Fieldsets and Legends:

- Group related form controls with <fieldset> and provide a description with <legend>.
- Example:

html

```
<fieldset>
  <legend>Personal Information</legend>
  <label for="fname">First Name:</label>
  <input type="text" id="fname" name="fname">

  <label for="lname">Last Name:</label>
  <input type="text" id="lname" name="lname">
</fieldset>
```

3.3 ARIA Attributes:

- Use ARIA attributes for advanced accessibility needs.
- Example:

html

```
<input type="text" name="search" aria-label="Search for products">
```

4. Styling Forms with CSS for Better Usability

Styling forms improves their appearance and usability, making them more engaging and easier to navigate.

4.1 Basic Styling:

- Use padding, margins, and borders to enhance readability.
- Example:

css

```css
input, select, textarea, button {
    font-size: 16px;
    margin: 10px 0;
    padding: 10px;
    border: 1px solid #ccc;
    border-radius: 4px;
}
```

4.2 Hover and Focus States:

- Provide visual feedback when users interact with form controls.

- Example:

css

```
input:focus {
    border-color: #007BFF;
    outline: none;
}

button:hover {
    background-color: #007BFF;
    color: #fff;
}
```

4.3 Responsive Forms:

- Use flexible layouts to ensure forms work on all devices.
- Example:

css

```
form {
    max-width: 600px;
    margin: 0 auto;
}
```

4.4 Styling Validation States:

- Highlight errors and successes using :valid and :invalid.
- Example:

css

```
input:invalid {
    border-color: red;
}

input:valid {
    border-color: green;
}
```

HTML5 forms are powerful tools for collecting user input, and they come with built-in validation and accessibility features. By combining the <form>, <input>, <textarea>, and <select> elements, you can create comprehensive and user-friendly forms. Styling forms with CSS enhances usability and provides a polished appearance. In the next chapter, we'll delve into advanced HTML5 features like the <canvas> and <svg> elements to add interactivity and graphics to your web pages. Let's continue building!

Chapter 8: Advanced HTML5 Features

1. Using the <canvas> Element for Graphics

The <canvas> element allows developers to draw graphics directly in the browser using JavaScript. It is commonly used for creating dynamic, interactive visuals like charts, games, and animations.

1.1 Basic Syntax of <canvas>:

- The <canvas> element creates a blank drawing area on a webpage.
- Attributes:
    - width: Specifies the canvas width (default is 300px).
    - height: Specifies the canvas height (default is 150px).
- Example:

html

```
<canvas id="myCanvas" width="400" height="300"></canvas>
```

1.2 Drawing on Canvas with JavaScript:

- To draw on the canvas, you need to access its 2D rendering context.

- Example: Drawing a rectangle

html

```
<script>
  const canvas = document.getElementById('myCanvas');
  const ctx = canvas.getContext('2d');

  // Draw a blue rectangle
  ctx.fillStyle = 'blue';
  ctx.fillRect(50, 50, 200, 100);
</script>
```

1.3 Advanced Canvas Features:

- Drawing lines:

javascript

```
ctx.beginPath();
ctx.moveTo(50, 50);
ctx.lineTo(250, 150);
ctx.stroke();
```

- Adding text:

javascript

```
ctx.font = '20px Arial';
ctx.fillText('Hello, Canvas!', 100, 50);
```

- Animations:
    - Use requestAnimationFrame for smooth animations.

---

2. The <svg> Element for Scalable Vector Graphics

SVG (Scalable Vector Graphics) allows you to create resolution-independent graphics that scale perfectly on all devices.

2.1 Basic Syntax of <svg>:

- The <svg> element contains XML-based graphics markup.
- Example:

html

```
<svg width="400" height="300">
    <circle cx="150" cy="150" r="100" fill="blue" />
</svg>
```

2.2 Common SVG Shapes:

- **Rectangle:**

html

```
<rect x="50" y="50" width="200" height="100" fill="red" />
```

- **Circle:**

  html

  ```
  <circle cx="150" cy="150" r="50" fill="green" />
  ```

- **Line:**

  html

  ```
  <line  x1="50"  y1="50"  x2="250"  y2="150"  stroke="black"  stroke-width="2" />
  ```

2.3 Combining SVG with CSS and JavaScript:

- Style SVG with CSS:

  html

  ```
  <style>
    circle {
        fill: yellow;
        stroke: black;
        stroke-width: 3;
    }
  </style>
  ```

- Add interactivity with JavaScript:

  javascript

```
const circle = document.querySelector('circle');
circle.addEventListener('click', () => {
    circle.setAttribute('fill', 'blue');
});
```

3. Offline Capabilities with <application> and Service Workers

HTML5 supports offline functionality, enabling websites to work without an internet connection.

3.1 Application Cache (Deprecated but Still Relevant):

- Use <application> to cache resources locally for offline use.
- Example:

html

```
<!DOCTYPE html>
<html manifest="example.appcache">
<head>
    <title>Offline App</title>
</head>
<body>
    <h1>This page works offline!</h1>
</body>
</html>
```

- **Manifest File (example.appcache):**

bash

```
CACHE MANIFEST
# List of files to cache
/index.html
/styles.css
/script.js
```

3.2 Service Workers (Modern Solution):

- Service workers are scripts that run in the background to manage offline caching and resource delivery.
- Example: Basic service worker setup

javascript

```
// Register the service worker
if ('serviceWorker' in navigator) {
    navigator.serviceWorker.register('/service-worker.js')
        .then(() => console.log('Service Worker Registered'));
}
```
javascript

```
// Inside service-worker.js
self.addEventListener('install', (event) => {
    event.waitUntil(
        caches.open('v1').then((cache) => {
```

```
      return cache.addAll(['/index.html', '/styles.css', '/script.js']);
    })
  );
});


self.addEventListener('fetch', (event) => {
  event.respondWith(
    caches.match(event.request).then((response) => {
      return response || fetch(event.request);
    })
  );
});
```

4. Geolocation and Web Storage APIs

HTML5 introduces APIs for geolocation and local storage, enhancing interactivity and functionality.

4.1 Geolocation API:

- Allows websites to retrieve a user's location (with their permission).
- Example: Retrieving location

javascript

```
if (navigator.geolocation) {
  navigator.geolocation.getCurrentPosition((position) => {
```

```
    console.log(`Latitude: ${position.coords.latitude}`);
    console.log(`Longitude: ${position.coords.longitude}`);
  });
} else {
  console.log('Geolocation is not supported by this browser.');
}
```

4.2 Web Storage API:

- Replaces cookies for client-side storage with two mechanisms:
  - **Local Storage:** Persists data even after the browser is closed.
  - **Session Storage:** Data is cleared when the session ends.

Using Local Storage:

- Save data:

  javascript

  ```
  localStorage.setItem('username', 'JohnDoe');
  ```

- Retrieve data:

  javascript

  ```
  const username = localStorage.getItem('username');
  ```

```
console.log(username);
```

Using Session Storage:

- Save data:

```javascript
sessionStorage.setItem('sessionID', '12345');
```

- Retrieve data:

```javascript
const sessionID = sessionStorage.getItem('sessionID');
console.log(sessionID);
```

Advanced HTML5 features like the <canvas> and <svg> elements allow developers to create rich graphics and interactive visuals. Offline capabilities with service workers enhance user experiences by enabling access without an internet connection, while the Geolocation and Web Storage APIs provide dynamic, personalized interactions. Mastering these tools opens the door to building sophisticated, modern web applications. In the next chapter, we'll explore the world of CSS3, starting with colors, fonts, and typography. Let's keep building!

Chapter 9: Introduction to CSS3

1. CSS Syntax and Selectors

CSS (Cascading Style Sheets) is used to style HTML elements, controlling the presentation of web pages, including layouts, colors, fonts, and spacing.

1.1 CSS Syntax:

- A CSS rule is made up of a **selector** and a **declaration block**.
- Example:

css

```
h1 {
    color: blue; /* Sets the text color to blue */
    font-size: 24px; /* Sets the font size */
}
```

- **Selector:** Targets the HTML element(s) (e.g., h1).
- **Property:** Defines what aspect of the element to style (e.g., color).
- **Value:** Specifies the style for the property (e.g., blue).

1.2 CSS Selectors: Selectors define which HTML elements a style applies to.

- **Type Selector:** Targets all elements of a specific type.

css

```
p {
    color: gray;
}
```

- **Class Selector:** Targets elements with a specific class attribute.

css

```
.highlight {
    background-color: yellow;
}
```

- **ID Selector:** Targets an element with a specific id attribute.

css

```
#main-title {
    text-align: center;
}
```

- **Group Selector:** Applies styles to multiple elements.

css

```
h1, h2, h3 {
    color: darkblue;
}
```

- **Descendant Selector:** Targets elements inside a specific container.

css

```
div p {
    margin: 10px;
}
```

---

2. Inline, Internal, and External CSS

CSS can be applied in three ways, each with its own use case and level of maintainability.

2.1 Inline CSS:

- Applied directly within an HTML element using the style attribute.
- Example:

html

```
<h1 style="color: red;">Inline Styled Heading</h1>
```

- **When to Use:** For quick, one-off styling changes.
- **Drawback:** Difficult to maintain and scales poorly.

2.2 Internal CSS:

- Defined within a <style> tag inside the <head> section.
- Example:

html

```
<head>
  <style>
    body {
      background-color: lightgray;
    }
  </style>
</head>
```

- **When to Use:** For small projects or single-page applications.
- **Drawback:** Not reusable across multiple pages.

2.3 External CSS:

- Defined in a separate .css file and linked to the HTML document using a <link> tag.

- Example:

html

```
<link rel="stylesheet" href="styles.css">
css

/* styles.css */
body {
    font-family: Arial, sans-serif;
}
```

- **When to Use:** For scalable and maintainable projects.
- **Benefit:** Ensures consistency across multiple pages.

---

3. The Importance of the Cascade and Specificity

3.1 The Cascade: The "cascade" determines how conflicting styles are resolved when multiple rules target the same element.

- **Order of Precedence:**
    1. Inline styles (highest priority).
    2. Internal and external styles, applied in order of appearance.
    3. Browser default styles (lowest priority).
- **Example:**

html

```
<style>
  p {
    color: blue; /* Internal CSS */
  }
</style>
<p style="color: red;">This text is red.</p>
```

3.2 Specificity: Specificity is a ranking system used to determine which CSS rule is applied when multiple rules conflict.

- **Hierarchy of Specificity:**
    1. Inline styles (style="...") = **1000**
    2. ID selectors (#id) = **100**
    3. Class selectors (.class), attributes, and pseudo-classes (:hover) = **10**
    4. Type selectors (div, p, h1) = **1**
- **Example:**

css

```
p {
   color: blue; /* Specificity = 1 */
}

.highlight {
   color: green; /* Specificity = 10 */
```

```
}

#special {
    color: red; /* Specificity = 100 */
}
html

<p id="special" class="highlight">This text is red.</p>
```

4. Understanding the Box Model

The box model describes how elements are displayed on the webpage, including their dimensions and spacing.

4.1 Components of the Box Model:

1. **Content:** The actual text or media inside the element.
2. **Padding:** Space between the content and the border.
3. **Border:** The boundary surrounding the element.
4. **Margin:** The space outside the border that separates the element from others.

4.2 Visual Representation:

lua

```
|-------------------------|
```

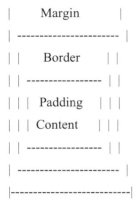

```
|      Margin       |
| --------------------- |
|  |    Border    | |
|  | ---------------- | |
|  | | Padding  | | |
|  | | Content  | | |
|  | ---------------- | |
| --------------------- |
|--------------------------|
```

4.3 CSS for the Box Model:

- Setting dimensions:

  css

  ```
  div {
      width: 200px;
      height: 100px;
  }
  ```

- Adding padding:

  css

  ```
  div {
      padding: 20px;
  }
  ```

- Adding a border:

css

```
div {
    border: 2px solid black;
}
```

- Adding margin:

css

```
div {
    margin: 10px;
}
```

4.4 Box-Sizing Property:

- The box-sizing property determines whether padding and border are included in an element's width and height.

    o Default (content-box): Padding and border are **not** included.

    o Alternative (border-box): Padding and border are included.

    o Example:

    css

    ```
    div {
        box-sizing: border-box;
    }
    ```

}

CSS3 introduces powerful tools for styling and enhancing web content. By mastering CSS syntax, selectors, and the box model, you lay a solid foundation for creating visually appealing and well-structured web pages. Understanding the cascade and specificity ensures consistent styling across your project. In the next chapter, we'll explore working with colors, fonts, and typography to bring your designs to life. Let's continue styling!

Chapter 10: Working with Colors, Fonts, and Typography

1. CSS Color Formats

Colors are vital in web design, affecting aesthetics, readability, and user experience. CSS offers multiple ways to define colors.

1.1 Hexadecimal Colors:

- A six-digit code representing the red, green, and blue (RGB) components of a color.
- Syntax: #RRGGBB
- Example:

css

```
body {
    background-color: #3498db; /* Light blue */
}
```

- Short form: #RGB (e.g., #FFF for white).

1.2 RGB Colors:

- Specifies colors as RGB values ranging from 0 to 255.
- Syntax: rgb(red, green, blue)
- Example:

css

```
h1 {
    color: rgb(52, 152, 219); /* Light blue */
}
```

- **RGBA (with transparency):**
  - Adds an alpha channel for opacity (0 = transparent, 1 = opaque).
  - Example:

    css

    ```
    div {
        background-color: rgba(52, 152, 219, 0.5); /* Semi-transparent light blue */
    }
    ```

1.3 HSL Colors:

- Defines colors using hue, saturation, and lightness.
- Syntax: hsl(hue, saturation%, lightness%)
- Example:

css

```
p {
    color: hsl(210, 50%, 60%); /* Light blue */
}
```

- **HSLA (with transparency):**
    - Example:

    css

    ```
    span {
        background-color: hsla(210, 50%, 60%, 0.3); /* Semi-
    transparent light blue */
    }
    ```

1.4 Named Colors:

- CSS includes predefined color names like red, blue, green, etc.
- Example:

css

```
a {
    color: tomato;
}
```

2. Custom Fonts with @font-face

The @font-face rule allows you to use custom fonts not available in the user's system.

2.1 Adding Custom Fonts:

- Download a font file (e.g., .woff or .ttf) and add it to your project.
- Example:

css

```css
@font-face {
    font-family: 'MyCustomFont';
    src: url('fonts/MyCustomFont.woff2') format('woff2'),
        url('fonts/MyCustomFont.ttf') format('truetype');
}

body {
    font-family: 'MyCustomFont', sans-serif;
}
```

2.2 Benefits of Custom Fonts:

- Consistency: Ensures the same font is displayed across all devices.
- Branding: Allows unique typography for your design.

3. Using Google Fonts and System Fonts

3.1 Google Fonts:

- Google Fonts is a free library of web fonts, easy to integrate into your project.

Steps to Use Google Fonts:

1. Visit Google Fonts.
2. Choose a font and copy the \<link\> code.
3. Add the link to your HTML \<head\> section.

   html

   ```
   <link
   href="https://fonts.googleapis.com/css2?family=Roboto:wght@400;700&display=swap" rel="stylesheet">
   ```

4. Apply the font in your CSS:

   css

   ```
   body {
       font-family: 'Roboto', sans-serif;
   }
   ```

3.2 System Fonts:

- System fonts are pre-installed on the user's device, ensuring fast load times.
- Example of a font stack:

css

```css
body {
    font-family: 'Segoe UI', Tahoma, Geneva, Verdana, sans-serif;
}
```

---

4. *Typography Best Practices for Readability*

Typography plays a key role in enhancing user experience. Here are some best practices to ensure readability and aesthetic appeal:

4.1 Font Sizes and Units:

- Use relative units (em, rem) for scalable typography.
    o Example:

css

```css
body {
    font-size: 16px; /* Base font size */
}
```

```css
h1 {
    font-size: 2rem; /* 2x the base font size */
}
```

4.2 Line Height:

- Maintain sufficient spacing between lines for readability.
- Ideal line height: 1.5 to 1.8 times the font size.

css

```css
p {
    line-height: 1.6;
}
```

4.3 Contrast:

- Ensure sufficient contrast between text and background for accessibility.
    - Example of accessible contrast:

    css

    ```css
    body {
        color: #333;
        background-color: #fff;
    }
    ```

4.4 Font Weights:

- Use lighter weights for body text and bold weights for headings.

css

```
h1 {
    font-weight: 700; /* Bold */
}

p {
    font-weight: 400; /* Regular */
}
```

4.5 Text Alignment:

- Use left-aligned text for readability (especially for long paragraphs).

css

```
p {
    text-align: left;
}
```

4.6 Responsive Typography:

- Use media queries to adjust font sizes for different screen sizes.

css

```
@media (max-width: 768px) {
  body {
    font-size: 14px;
  }
}
```

4.7 Avoid Overusing Fonts:

- Stick to two or three font families to maintain a clean design.

CSS3 provides powerful tools for working with colors, fonts, and typography to enhance the visual appeal and readability of web pages. By mastering CSS color formats, custom fonts, and typography best practices, you can create aesthetically pleasing and accessible designs. In the next chapter, we'll explore CSS layout techniques, starting with the foundational box model and progressing to modern layout methods like Flexbox and Grid. Let's continue styling!

Chapter 11: Layout Basics with CSS3

1. Understanding Block, Inline, and Inline-Block Elements

CSS layout behavior depends heavily on the display type of elements.

1.1 Block Elements:

- Occupy the full width of their parent container by default.
- Start on a new line.
- Examples: <div>, <p>, <h1>, <section>.
- Example:

html

```
<div style="background-color: lightblue;">This is a block element.</div>
```

Behavior:

- Takes up 100% of the width unless styled otherwise.

css

```
div {
    width: 50%;
    margin: auto;
```

}

1.2 Inline Elements:

- Occupy only as much width as their content.
- Do not start on a new line.
- Examples: <span>, <a>, <strong>, <em>.
- Example:

html

```
<span style="background-color: lightcoral;">This is an inline element.</span>
```

Behavior:

- Cannot have width, height, or vertical margins set.

1.3 Inline-Block Elements:

- Behave like inline elements but allow width, height, and margin styling.
- Example:

html

```
<div style="display: inline-block; width: 100px; height: 50px; background-color: lightgreen;">
```

This is inline-block.

</div>

Use Case:

- Useful for layouts requiring precise sizing and alignment.

---

2. Positioning: Static, Relative, Absolute, and Fixed

CSS positioning determines how elements are placed in the document.

2.1 Static Positioning (Default):

- Elements appear in the normal document flow.
- Example:

css

```css
div {
    position: static;
}
```

2.2 Relative Positioning:

- Positioned relative to its normal position.
- Example:

css

```
div {
    position: relative;
    top: 20px;
    left: 10px;
}
```

- **Effect:** Moves the element but leaves its original space intact.

2.3 Absolute Positioning:

- Positioned relative to the nearest positioned ancestor.
- Example:

css

```
div {
    position: absolute;
    top: 50px;
    left: 30px;
}
```

- **Effect:** Removed from normal flow and does not reserve space.

2.4 Fixed Positioning:

- Positioned relative to the browser window and does not move with scrolling.
- Example:

css

```
div {
    position: fixed;
    bottom: 10px;
    right: 20px;
}
```

- **Use Case:** Sticky headers or footers.

---

3. Controlling Overflow and z-index

3.1 Overflow:

- Defines how content exceeding an element's dimensions is handled.
- Values:
  - visible: Default; content spills out of the element.
  - hidden: Clips the content.
  - scroll: Adds scrollbars.
  - auto: Adds scrollbars only when necessary.
- Example:

css

```
div {
    width: 200px;
    height: 100px;
    overflow: scroll;
}
```

3.2 z-index:

- Controls the stack order of overlapping elements.
- Higher z-index values appear on top.
- Example:

css

```
div {
    position: absolute;
    z-index: 10;
}
```

- **Use Case:** Layering tooltips, modals, or dropdown menus.

4. Using Floats and Clearfix for Layout

Floats were an early method of creating multi-column layouts before Flexbox and Grid became widely used.

4.1 Floats:

- Float elements to the left or right of their container.
- Example:

css

```css
.left {
    float: left;
    width: 50%;
}

.right {
    float: right;
    width: 50%;
}
```

- HTML:

html

```html
<div class="left">Left Content</div>
<div class="right">Right Content</div>
```

4.2 Clearfix:

- Floating elements can cause container collapse if not cleared.

- The clearfix hack forces the parent container to wrap its floated children.

CSS Clearfix Example:

css

```
.container::after {
    content: "";
    display: table;
    clear: both;
}
```

HTML Example:

html

```
<div class="container">
    <div class="left">Left Content</div>
    <div class="right">Right Content</div>
</div>
```

Understanding the basics of CSS layout with block, inline, and inline-block elements, positioning, and overflow handling is crucial for creating structured and visually appealing web pages. While floats and clearfix were once the standard for layouts, they have been largely replaced by modern techniques like Flexbox and Grid, which will be explored in the next chapters. Let's dive deeper into advanced layout techniques to enhance your web design!

Chapter 12: Modern Layouts with Flexbox

---

1. Introduction to Flexbox and Its Properties

The CSS Flexible Box Layout, or Flexbox, is a powerful layout model designed for distributing and aligning elements efficiently, even when their sizes are dynamic.

1.1 Why Use Flexbox?

- Simplifies creating responsive layouts.
- Provides precise control over alignment, spacing, and order of elements.
- Eliminates the need for older layout techniques like floats and clearfix hacks.

1.2 Flexbox Terminology:

- **Flex Container:** The parent element with display: flex.
- **Flex Items:** The direct children of a flex container.

1.3 Enabling Flexbox:

- Set display: flex on a container to enable Flexbox for its children.

css

```
.container {
    display: flex;
}
```

1.4 Key Properties of Flexbox:

1. **Flex Container Properties:**
   - flex-direction: Defines the direction of items.
     - Values: row (default), row-reverse, column, column-reverse.

   css

   ```
   .container {
       flex-direction: row;
   }
   ```

   - justify-content: Aligns items along the main axis.
     - Values: flex-start, flex-end, center, space-between, space-around, space-evenly.

   css

```css
.container {
    justify-content: space-between;
}
```

- o align-items: Aligns items along the cross axis.
  - Values: stretch (default), flex-start, flex-end, center, baseline.

css

```css
.container {
    align-items: center;
}
```

- o flex-wrap: Allows items to wrap onto multiple lines.
  - Values: nowrap (default), wrap, wrap-reverse.

css

```css
.container {
    flex-wrap: wrap;
}
```

2. Flex Item Properties:

- o flex-grow: Defines how much an item grows relative to others.

css

```css
.item {
```

```
flex-grow: 1;
}
```

o   flex-shrink: Defines how much an item shrinks relative to others.

css

```
.item {
   flex-shrink: 1;
}
```

o   flex-basis: Sets the initial size of an item before space distribution.

css

```
.item {
   flex-basis: 200px;
}
```

o   align-self: Overrides align-items for individual items.

css

```
.item {
   align-self: flex-end;
}
```

2. Creating Responsive Layouts with Flexbox

Flexbox excels at creating layouts that adapt to different screen sizes.

2.1 Basic Responsive Layout:

- Example: Three columns that stack on smaller screens.

html

```
<div class="container">
  <div class="item">Column 1</div>
  <div class="item">Column 2</div>
  <div class="item">Column 3</div>
</div>
```

css

```
.container {
  display: flex;
  flex-wrap: wrap;
}

.item {
  flex: 1 1 30%; /* Grow, shrink, and basis */
  margin: 10px;
}

@media (max-width: 768px) {
  .item {
    flex: 1 1 100%;
  }
}
```

}

2.2 Nested Flex Containers:

* Flexbox can nest containers for complex layouts.

html

```
<div class="parent">
   <div class="child">
      <div class="nested">Nested Item</div>
   </div>
</div>
```

css

```
.parent {
   display: flex;
}

.child {
   display: flex;
   flex: 1;
   justify-content: center;
   align-items: center;
}
```

3. Aligning and Distributing Content in a Flexible Container

Flexbox makes it easy to align and distribute content.

3.1 Aligning Items Along the Main Axis:

- Use justify-content to position items along the main axis.

css

```
.container {
    display: flex;
    justify-content: space-evenly;
}
```

3.2 Aligning Items Along the Cross Axis:

- Use align-items to position items along the cross axis.

css

```
.container {
    display: flex;
    align-items: stretch;
}
```

3.3 Aligning Individual Items:

- Use align-self to override alignment for a specific item.

css

```
.item {
    align-self: center;
```

```
}
```

3.4 Centering Content:

- Flexbox simplifies centering both horizontally and vertically.

css

```css
.container {
    display: flex;
    justify-content: center;
    align-items: center;
    height: 100vh;
}
```

4. Real-World Examples of Flexbox Usage

4.1 Navigation Bar:

- Example:

html

```html
<nav class="navbar">
    <div class="logo">Logo</div>
    <ul class="nav-links">
        <li>Home</li>
        <li>About</li>
        <li>Contact</li>
    </ul>
```

```
</nav>
css
```

```css
.navbar {
    display: flex;
    justify-content: space-between;
    align-items: center;
    padding: 10px 20px;
}

.nav-links {
    display: flex;
    list-style: none;
}

.nav-links li {
    margin: 0 10px;
}
```

4.2 Card Layout:

- Example:

html

```html
<div class="cards">
    <div class="card">Card 1</div>
    <div class="card">Card 2</div>
    <div class="card">Card 3</div>
</div>
```

css

```css
.cards {
  display: flex;
  flex-wrap: wrap;
  gap: 20px;
}

.card {
  flex: 1 1 calc(33.333% - 20px);
  background-color: lightblue;
  padding: 20px;
}
```

4.3 Footer Layout:

- Example:

html

```html
<footer class="footer">
  <div>About Us</div>
  <div>Links</div>
  <div>Contact</div>
</footer>
```

css

```css
.footer {
  display: flex;
  justify-content: space-around;
```

```
    padding: 20px;
    background-color: #333;
    color: white;
}
```

Flexbox is a versatile and efficient tool for creating modern, responsive web layouts. By mastering its properties and techniques, you can handle alignment, distribution, and responsiveness with ease. In the next chapter, we'll explore CSS Grid, which offers even greater control for building complex layouts. Let's continue designing!

Chapter 13: Advanced Layouts with CSS Grid

1. Introduction to CSS Grid and Its Properties

CSS Grid is a powerful layout system designed for two-dimensional layouts, allowing developers to manage rows and columns simultaneously.

1.1 Why Use CSS Grid?

- Provides precise control over both horizontal and vertical alignment.
- Simplifies the creation of complex layouts like grids, galleries, and multi-section pages.

1.2 Enabling CSS Grid:

- Set display: grid on a container to enable Grid layout for its children.

css

.grid-container {

```
    display: grid;
}
```

1.3 Key Properties of CSS Grid:

1. **Grid Container Properties:**
   - o grid-template-rows: Defines row sizes.

     css

     grid-template-rows: 100px auto 50px;

   - o grid-template-columns: Defines column sizes.

     css

     grid-template-columns: 1fr 2fr 1fr;

   - o gap: Adds spacing between rows and columns.

     css

     gap: 10px;

2. **Grid Item Properties:**
   - o grid-column: Specifies the start and end columns for an item.

     css

grid-column: 1 / 3;

    o   grid-row: Specifies the start and end rows for an item.

css

grid-row: 2 / 4;

---

2. Defining Rows, Columns, and Grid Areas

2.1 Defining Rows and Columns:

- Use grid-template-rows and grid-template-columns to define the structure.

css

```
.grid-container {
    display: grid;
    grid-template-rows: 100px 200px;
    grid-template-columns: 1fr 2fr;
}
```

Example:

html

```
<div class="grid-container">
    <div class="item">Item 1</div>
```

```
<div class="item">Item 2</div>
<div class="item">Item 3</div>
</div>
```

Result:

- Two rows: First row is 100px, second is 200px.
- Two columns: First column takes one fraction (1fr), second takes two fractions (2fr).

2.2 Naming and Defining Grid Areas:

- Assign names to grid areas using grid-template-areas.
- Example:

css

```
.grid-container {
    display: grid;
    grid-template-areas:
        "header header"
        "sidebar content"
        "footer footer";
    grid-template-rows: 100px auto 50px;
    grid-template-columns: 200px 1fr;
}

.header {
    grid-area: header;
```

```
        }

        .sidebar {
            grid-area: sidebar;
        }

        .content {
            grid-area: content;
        }

        .footer {
            grid-area: footer;
        }
```

HTML:

html

```
<div class="grid-container">
    <div class="header">Header</div>
    <div class="sidebar">Sidebar</div>
    <div class="content">Content</div>
    <div class="footer">Footer</div>
</div>
```

Result:

- A layout with a header, sidebar, main content area, and footer.

3. Combining CSS Grid and Flexbox

While CSS Grid excels at creating overall page layouts, Flexbox is ideal for aligning and distributing items within a container. The two can be used together for optimal results.

Example: Combining CSS Grid and Flexbox:

1. Use Grid for the overall structure.
2. Use Flexbox for aligning content within individual grid items.

HTML:

html

```
<div class="grid-container">
   <header class="header">Header</header>
   <nav class="sidebar">Sidebar</nav>
   <main class="content">
      <div class="flex-item">Flex Item 1</div>
      <div class="flex-item">Flex Item 2</div>
   </main>
   <footer class="footer">Footer</footer>
</div>
```

CSS:

css

```
.grid-container {
    display: grid;
    grid-template-areas:
        "header header"
        "sidebar content"
        "footer footer";
    grid-template-columns: 200px 1fr;
    grid-template-rows: 100px auto 50px;
}


.content {
    display: flex;
    flex-direction: column;
    align-items: center;
    justify-content: center;
}
```

4. Building a Complete Website Layout with CSS Grid

HTML Structure:

html

```
<div class="grid-container">
    <header class="header">Header</header>
    <nav class="sidebar">Sidebar</nav>
    <main class="content">Main Content</main>
    <footer class="footer">Footer</footer>
</div>
```

CSS:

css

```
.grid-container {
    display: grid;
    grid-template-areas:
        "header header"
        "sidebar content"
        "footer footer";
    grid-template-rows: 100px auto 50px;
    grid-template-columns: 200px 1fr;
    gap: 10px;
}

.header {
    grid-area: header;
    background-color: lightblue;
    text-align: center;
    padding: 10px;
}

.sidebar {
    grid-area: sidebar;
    background-color: lightgray;
    padding: 10px;
}

.content {
    grid-area: content;
    background-color: white;
```

```
  padding: 20px;
}

.footer {
  grid-area: footer;
  background-color: lightblue;
  text-align: center;
  padding: 10px;
}
```

CSS Grid revolutionizes web layout design by providing precise control over rows, columns, and grid areas. By combining Grid with Flexbox, you can handle complex designs with ease, building fully responsive, professional-looking layouts. In the next chapter, we'll explore responsive design techniques, focusing on media queries and other strategies to ensure your layouts work seamlessly across devices. Let's continue designing!

Chapter 14: Responsive Design with Media Queries

1. The Concept of Responsive Web Design

Responsive web design ensures that a website looks and functions well across different devices and screen sizes. This approach adapts layouts, fonts, images, and other elements to provide an optimal user experience.

1.1 Why Responsive Design Matters:

- **Device Diversity:** Users access websites on desktops, tablets, and smartphones with varying screen sizes.
- **Improved User Experience:** Ensures content is accessible and legible without excessive zooming or scrolling.
- **SEO Benefits:** Search engines prioritize mobile-friendly sites in their rankings.

1.2 Key Principles of Responsive Design:

1. **Fluid Grids:** Use flexible layouts that adjust based on the viewport size.

2. **Flexible Media:** Ensure images and videos scale proportionally.

3. **Media Queries:** Apply CSS rules specific to certain screen sizes.

2. Writing Media Queries for Different Screen Sizes

Media queries enable developers to define CSS rules that apply based on device characteristics, such as screen width or orientation.

2.1 Basic Syntax:

css

```
@media (condition) {
   /* Styles here */
}
```

Example:

css

```
@media (max-width: 768px) {
   body {
      font-size: 14px;
   }
}
```

2.2 Common Breakpoints: Breakpoints are screen widths where the layout changes for better usability.

1. **Small Devices (Smartphones):**

    css

    ```
    @media (max-width: 480px) {
       /* Styles for smartphones */
    }
    ```

2. **Medium Devices (Tablets):**

    css

    ```
    @media (min-width: 481px) and (max-width: 768px) {
       /* Styles for tablets */
    }
    ```

3. **Large Devices (Desktops):**

    css

    ```
    @media (min-width: 769px) {
       /* Styles for desktops */
    }
    ```

2.3 Orientation Media Queries:

*   Apply styles based on device orientation.

- Example:

css

```
@media (orientation: portrait) {
  body {
    background-color: lightblue;
  }
}

@media (orientation: landscape) {
  body {
    background-color: lightgreen;
  }
}
```

3. Using Relative Units *(%, em, rem)* for Responsiveness

Relative units provide flexibility in sizing elements, allowing them to adapt to the viewport size.

3.1 Percentages (%):

- Use percentages for widths and heights relative to the parent container.
- Example:

css

```
.container {
    width: 80%; /* 80% of the parent container */
}
```

3.2 em Units:

- Relative to the font size of the parent element.
- Example:

css

```
p {
    font-size: 1.2em; /* 1.2 times the parent font size */
}
```

3.3 rem Units:

- Relative to the root font size (<html> element).
- Example:

css

```
html {
    font-size: 16px;
}

h1 {
```

```
    font-size: 2rem; /* 32px */
}
```

Why Use rem Over em?

- rem ensures consistency across nested elements, while em compounds sizes.

---

4. Designing for Mobile-First and Progressive Enhancement

4.1 Mobile-First Design:

- Start designing for smaller screens and scale up for larger devices.
- Define base styles for mobile devices, then add media queries for larger screens.

Example:

css

```css
/* Base styles for mobile devices */
body {
    font-size: 14px;
}

/* Larger screens (tablets) */
@media (min-width: 768px) {
```

```
  body {
    font-size: 16px;
  }
}

/* Desktops */
@media (min-width: 1024px) {
  body {
    font-size: 18px;
  }
}
```

4.2 Progressive Enhancement:

- Focus on core functionality first, then add advanced features for devices that support them.

Steps:

1. Ensure the website works on all devices with minimal styling.
2. Add styles and features for modern devices using media queries and advanced CSS.

---

5. Responsive Design Example:

HTML Structure:

html

```html
<div class="container">
   <header class="header">Header</header>
   <main class="content">Content</main>
   <footer class="footer">Footer</footer>
</div>
```

CSS Styles:

css

```css
/* Base styles (mobile-first) */
.container {
   display: flex;
   flex-direction: column;
   padding: 10px;
}

.header, .content, .footer {
   padding: 20px;
   text-align: center;
}

/* Tablets */
@media (min-width: 768px) {
   .container {
      flex-direction: row;
   }
}
```

```css
.header, .content, .footer {
    flex: 1;
}
}


/* Desktops */
@media (min-width: 1024px) {
    .container {
        max-width: 1200px;
        margin: 0 auto;
    }

    .header {
        flex: 2;
    }
}
```

Responsive design ensures websites are adaptable, accessible, and user-friendly on all devices. By mastering media queries, relative units, and mobile-first design, you can build layouts that seamlessly transition across screen sizes. In the next chapter, we'll explore enhancing interactivity and animations with CSS3, further enriching the user experience. Let's continue designing!

Chapter 15: CSS3 Transitions and Animations

---

1. Creating Smooth Transitions with transition

CSS transitions allow you to change property values smoothly over a specified duration.

1.1 Syntax of transition:

css

```
selector {
    transition: property duration timing-function delay;
}
```

- **Property:** The CSS property to animate (e.g., color, background-color, transform).
- **Duration:** The time the transition takes (e.g., 0.5s, 200ms).
- **Timing Function:** Defines the speed curve (e.g., ease, linear, ease-in, ease-out).
- **Delay:** Specifies when the transition starts (e.g., 1s).

1.2 Example: Button Hover Effect

html

```
<button class="btn">Hover Me</button>
```

css

```
.btn {
    background-color: lightblue;
    color: black;
    padding: 10px 20px;
    border: none;
    border-radius: 5px;
    transition: background-color 0.3s ease, color 0.3s ease;
}

.btn:hover {
    background-color: darkblue;
    color: white;
}
```

Result: The button smoothly changes color when hovered.

1.3 Transitioning Multiple Properties:

css

```
.box {
    width: 100px;
    height: 100px;
    background-color: lightcoral;
    transition: all 0.5s ease;
```

```
}

.box:hover {
    width: 150px;
    height: 150px;
    background-color: lightgreen;
}
```

2. Using @keyframes for CSS Animations

CSS animations allow you to define complex animations using the @keyframes rule.

2.1 Syntax of @keyframes:

css

```
@keyframes animation-name {
    0% {
        property: value;
    }
    100% {
        property: value;
    }
}
```

Example: Bounce Effect

html

```
<div class="ball"></div>
```

css

```css
.ball {
    width: 50px;
    height: 50px;
    background-color: red;
    border-radius: 50%;
    animation: bounce 2s infinite;
}

@keyframes bounce {
    0%, 100% {
        transform: translateY(0);
    }
    50% {
        transform: translateY(-100px);
    }
}
```

Result: The ball moves up and down repeatedly.

2.2 Animation Properties:

- animation-name: Name of the @keyframes animation.
- animation-duration: How long the animation takes.
- animation-timing-function: Speed curve (ease, linear, etc.).
- animation-delay: Time before the animation starts.

- animation-iteration-count: Number of repetitions (infinite for endless looping).
- animation-direction: Direction of the animation (normal, reverse, alternate).

Combining Properties:

css

```
.ball {
    animation: bounce 2s ease-in-out infinite alternate;
}
```

3. Best Practices for Performance-Optimized Animations

Animations can impact performance, especially on mobile devices. Follow these best practices:

3.1 Use GPU-Accelerated Properties:

- Prefer animating transform and opacity for smoother performance.
- Avoid animating properties like width, height, or box-shadow when possible.

3.2 Minimize Animation Layers:

- Keep animations simple to reduce browser processing.

3.3 Reduce Animation Duration and Iterations:

- Limit excessive animations to improve usability.

3.4 Use Hardware-Accelerated CSS:

- Use will-change to inform the browser about upcoming changes:

css

```css
.box {
    will-change: transform, opacity;
}
```

---

4. Real-World Use Cases: Hover Effects, Loaders, and More

4.1 Hover Effects:

- Example: Card Zoom Effect

html

```html
<div class="card">Hover Me</div>
```

css

```css
.card {
    width: 200px;
    height: 300px;
    background-color: lightgray;
    transition: transform 0.3s ease;
}

.card:hover {
    transform: scale(1.1);
}
```

4.2 Loading Spinners:

- Example: Rotating Loader

html

```html
<div class="loader"></div>
```

css

```css
.loader {
    width: 50px;
    height: 50px;
    border: 5px solid lightgray;
    border-top: 5px solid blue;
    border-radius: 50%;
    animation: spin 1s linear infinite;
}
```

```
@keyframes spin {
  from {
    transform: rotate(0deg);
  }
  to {
    transform: rotate(360deg);
  }
}
```

4.3 Button Animations:

- Example: Pulsing Button

html

```
<button class="pulse-btn">Click Me</button>
```
css

```
.pulse-btn {
  background-color: darkorange;
  color: white;
  padding: 10px 20px;
  border: none;
  border-radius: 5px;
  animation: pulse 1.5s infinite;
}

@keyframes pulse {
  0%, 100% {
```

```
    transform: scale(1);
  }
  50% {
    transform: scale(1.1);
  }
}
```

4.4 Hero Section Animations:

- Example: Fade-In Text

html

```html
<div class="hero-text">Welcome to Our Website</div>
```
css

```css
.hero-text {
  opacity: 0;
  animation: fadeIn 2s ease-in-out forwards;
}

@keyframes fadeIn {
  to {
    opacity: 1;
  }
}
```

CSS3 transitions and animations bring dynamic interactions and visual appeal to your website. By mastering transition and @keyframes, you can create smooth hover effects, engaging loaders, and other interactive elements. Focus on performance optimization to ensure your animations are fast and responsive. In the next chapter, we'll dive into CSS pseudo-classes and pseudo-elements for advanced styling techniques. Let's keep animating!

Chapter 16: Pseudo-Classes and Pseudo-Elements

1. Understanding Pseudo-Classes

Pseudo-classes define the special states of an element, allowing you to style elements dynamically based on their state or position.

1.1 Commonly Used Pseudo-Classes:

1. **:hover:**

   o Styles an element when the mouse pointer hovers over it.

   o Example:

   css

   ```css
   a:hover {
      color: blue;
      text-decoration: underline;
   }
   ```

2. **:focus:**

   o Styles an element when it receives focus (e.g., via tabbing or clicking).

o Example:

css

```
input:focus {
    border-color: lightblue;
    outline: none;
}
```

3. **:nth-child:**

o Targets elements based on their position among siblings.

o Example: Style every odd row in a table.

css

```
tr:nth-child(odd) {
    background-color: lightgray;
}
```

4. **:not:**

o Excludes elements that match the selector inside.

o Example:

css

```
p:not(.special) {
    color: gray;
}
```

5. **:first-child and :last-child:**

    o   Targets the first or last child of a parent element.

    o   Example:

css

```
li:first-child {
    font-weight: bold;
}

li:last-child {
    font-style: italic;
}
```

1.2 Pseudo-Class Example: Highlighting Active Navigation Link

html

```
<ul>
    <li><a href="#" class="active">Home</a></li>
    <li><a href="#">About</a></li>
    <li><a href="#">Contact</a></li>
</ul>
```
css

```
a.active {
    color: red;
    font-weight: bold;
}
```

2. Styling Content with Pseudo-Elements

Pseudo-elements are used to style specific parts of an element or insert content dynamically.

2.1 Commonly Used Pseudo-Elements:

1. **::before:**
   - o Inserts content before an element's content.
   - o Example:

     css

     ```
     h1::before {
         content: "★ ";
         color: gold;
     }
     ```

2. **::after:**
   - o Inserts content after an element's content.
   - o Example:

     css

     ```
     h1::after {
         content: " ★";
         color: gold;
     ```

}

3. **::first-letter:**

   o Styles the first letter of a text block.

   o Example:

   css

   ```css
   p::first-letter {
       font-size: 2em;
       color: red;
   }
   ```

4. **::first-line:**

   o Styles the first line of text in a block.

   o Example:

   css

   ```css
   p::first-line {
       font-weight: bold;
   }
   ```

2.2 Example: Decorative Quotation Marks

html

```html
<blockquote>
    This is a blockquote with decorative quotation marks.
```

```
</blockquote>
css


blockquote::before {
    content: "“";
    font-size: 2em;
    color: gray;
}


blockquote::after {
    content: "”";
    font-size: 2em;
    color: gray;
}
```

---

3. Combining Pseudo-Classes and Pseudo-Elements for Creative Effects

By combining pseudo-classes and pseudo-elements, you can create visually engaging effects.

3.1 Example: Stylish Buttons

html

```
<button class="btn">Hover Me</button>
css


.btn {
```

```css
    position: relative;
    padding: 10px 20px;
    background-color: lightblue;
    border: none;
    color: white;
    overflow: hidden;
    cursor: pointer;
}

.btn::before {
    content: "";
    position: absolute;
    top: 0;
    left: -100%;
    width: 100%;
    height: 100%;
    background-color: darkblue;
    transition: left 0.3s ease;
    z-index: 0;
}

.btn:hover::before {
    left: 0;
}

.btn {
    position: relative;
    z-index: 1;
}
```

3.2 Example: Notification Badges

html

```
<div class="notification">Messages</div>
```
css

```
.notification {
    position: relative;
    padding: 10px 20px;
    background-color: lightgray;
    border-radius: 5px;
}

.notification::after {
    content: "3";
    position: absolute;
    top: 5px;
    right: 5px;
    background-color: red;
    color: white;
    font-size: 0.8em;
    padding: 2px 5px;
    border-radius: 50%;
}
```

3.3 Example: Custom Underline on Hover

html

```html
<a href="#" class="link">Hover Over Me</a>
```
css

```css
.link {
    position: relative;
    color: blue;
    text-decoration: none;
}

.link::after {
    content: "";
    position: absolute;
    left: 0;
    bottom: -2px;
    width: 100%;
    height: 2px;
    background-color: blue;
    transform: scaleX(0);
    transition: transform 0.3s ease;
}

.link:hover::after {
    transform: scaleX(1);
}
```

Pseudo-classes and pseudo-elements are powerful tools for adding interactivity and enhancing the visual appeal of your website without extra markup. Mastering their use allows you to create dynamic effects and enrich user experiences. In the next chapter, we'll explore working with CSS variables and custom properties to make your stylesheets more efficient and maintainable. Let's continue styling!

Chapter 17: Working with CSS Variables

1. Declaring and Using CSS Variables

CSS variables, also called custom properties, are reusable values for properties like colors, fonts, and spacing. They make stylesheets more maintainable and dynamic.

1.1 Syntax of CSS Variables:

- Variables are defined using the -- prefix and are accessible within the :root or any specific selector.

Declaring a Variable:

css

```css
:root {
    --primary-color: #3498db;
    --secondary-color: #2ecc71;
    --font-size-large: 1.5rem;
}
```

Using a Variable:

- Use the var() function to reference a variable.

css

```
h1 {
    color: var(--primary-color);
    font-size: var(--font-size-large);
}
```

Fallback Value:

- Provide a fallback if the variable is not defined.

css

```
h1 {
    color: var(--primary-color, black);
}
```

1.2 Scope of Variables:

- Variables can be scoped globally (using :root) or locally to specific elements.

css

```
:root {
    --global-color: #555;
}

.container {
    --local-color: #333;
    color: var(--local-color);
```

}

---

2. The Advantages of CSS Variables Over Preprocessor Variables

CSS variables are often compared to preprocessor variables (like those in Sass or LESS), but they offer several unique advantages:

2.1 Runtime Changes:

- CSS variables can be updated dynamically with JavaScript, unlike preprocessor variables.
- Example:

html

```
<button onclick="changeTheme()">Change Theme</button>
```
css

```
:root {
    --primary-color: #3498db;
}

body {
    background-color: var(--primary-color);
}
```
javascript

```
function changeTheme() {
```

```
document.documentElement.style.setProperty('--primary-color',
'#e74c3c');
}
```

2.2 Native Browser Support:

- CSS variables are directly supported by browsers, while preprocessor variables require compilation.

2.3 Contextual Variables:

- CSS variables inherit and adapt based on their scope, making them more flexible for dynamic styling.

css

```css
.card {
  --card-border: 2px solid var(--primary-color);
  border: var(--card-border);
}
```

3. Using Variables for Theming and Maintaining Consistency
CSS variables simplify theming and ensure consistency across large projects.

3.1 Theming with Variables:

- Define variables for primary design elements like colors, fonts, and spacing.

Example: Light and Dark Theme:

css

```css
:root {
   --background-color: white;
   --text-color: black;
}

body.dark-mode {
   --background-color: black;
   --text-color: white;
}

body {
   background-color: var(--background-color);
   color: var(--text-color);
}
```

Switching Themes:

javascript

```javascript
document.body.classList.toggle('dark-mode');
```

3.2 Maintaining Design Consistency:

- Use variables to centralize key design properties.

Example: Button Design:

css

```css
:root {
    --button-padding: 10px 20px;
    --button-border-radius: 5px;
    --button-color: #3498db;
}

button {
    padding: var(--button-padding);
    border-radius: var(--button-border-radius);
    background-color: var(--button-color);
    color: white;
    border: none;
    cursor: pointer;
}
```

Updating Variables for All Buttons:

- Changing --button-color in :root automatically updates all buttons.

3.3 Responsive Design with Variables:

- Variables can adapt to different screen sizes using media queries.

Example:

css

```
:root {
    --font-size: 16px;
}

@media (max-width: 768px) {
    :root {
        --font-size: 14px;
    }
}

body {
    font-size: var(--font-size);
}
```

---

4. Real-World Example: Creating a Theme System
HTML:

html

```
<button onclick="setTheme('light')">Light Theme</button>
<button onclick="setTheme('dark')">Dark Theme</button>
<div class="card">Themed Content</div>
```

CSS:

css

```css
:root {
  --background-color: white;
  --text-color: black;
  --card-background: #f5f5f5;
}


body {
  background-color: var(--background-color);
  color: var(--text-color);
}


.card {
  background-color: var(--card-background);
  padding: 20px;
  border-radius: 5px;
}


body.dark-mode {
  --background-color: black;
  --text-color: white;
  --card-background: #333;
}
```

JavaScript:

javascript

```javascript
function setTheme(theme) {
  if (theme === 'dark') {
    document.body.classList.add('dark-mode');
  } else {
    document.body.classList.remove('dark-mode');
```

```
    }
}
```

Result: The theme dynamically changes based on user input.

CSS variables bring powerful flexibility to web design, making stylesheets easier to maintain and adapt. They outperform preprocessor variables by enabling runtime updates and inheriting scope naturally. Using variables for theming, responsiveness, and consistency simplifies project management and enhances user experience. In the next chapter, we'll explore integrating CSS with JavaScript for even greater interactivity. Let's keep building!

Chapter 18: Introduction to JavaScript for HTML5 and CSS3

---

1. Basics of JavaScript to Enhance HTML and CSS

JavaScript is a powerful scripting language that adds interactivity and functionality to HTML5 and CSS3.

1.1 Key Features of JavaScript:

- **Dynamic Behavior:** Modify HTML content and CSS styles dynamically.
- **Event Handling:** Respond to user interactions like clicks, hovers, and inputs.
- **Control Structures:** Use loops, conditions, and functions for logic.
- **Cross-Platform:** Runs directly in the browser, no need for compilation.

1.2 Basic Syntax and Concepts:

javascript

// Variables

```
let message = "Hello, World!";
const PI = 3.14;

// Functions
function greet(name) {
    return `Hello, ${name}`;
}

// Event Handling
document.querySelector("button").addEventListener("click", () => {
    alert("Button clicked!");
});
```

1.3 Linking JavaScript to HTML:

- Add JavaScript with the <script> tag.
- Example:

    html

    ```
    <script>
        console.log("Inline JavaScript Example");
    </script>
    ```

- External File:

    html

    ```
    <script src="script.js"></script>
    ```

2. Manipulating the DOM with JavaScript

The DOM (Document Object Model) represents the structure of an HTML document. JavaScript interacts with the DOM to modify or retrieve elements and content.

2.1 Selecting Elements:

- getElementById: Selects an element by its ID.

  javascript

  ```javascript
  const heading = document.getElementById("title");
  ```

- querySelector: Selects the first matching element.

  javascript

  ```javascript
  const button = document.querySelector(".btn");
  ```

- querySelectorAll: Selects all matching elements.

  javascript

  ```javascript
  const items = document.querySelectorAll(".item");
  ```

2.2 Changing Content:

- Modify text:

  javascript

  ```
  heading.textContent = "New Title";
  ```

- Modify HTML:

  javascript

  ```
  heading.innerHTML = "<span>Styled Title</span>";
  ```

2.3 Changing Styles:

- Inline styles:

  javascript

  ```
  heading.style.color = "blue";
  heading.style.fontSize = "24px";
  ```

- Add/Remove classes:

  javascript

  ```
  heading.classList.add("highlight");
  heading.classList.remove("highlight");
  ```

2.4 Adding and Removing Elements:

- Create an element:

javascript

```
const newDiv = document.createElement("div");
newDiv.textContent = "New Content";
document.body.appendChild(newDiv);
```

- Remove an element:

javascript

```
const oldDiv = document.querySelector(".old");
oldDiv.remove();
```

---

3. Integrating JavaScript for Interactivity

JavaScript adds interactivity to a webpage, such as dropdown menus, modals, and more.

3.1 Dropdown Menu:

html

```
<button class="dropdown-btn">Menu</button>
<div class="dropdown-content" style="display: none;">Dropdown Content</div>
```
javascript

```
const button = document.querySelector(".dropdown-btn");
const content = document.querySelector(".dropdown-content");

button.addEventListener("click", () => {
    content.style.display = content.style.display === "none" ? "block" : "none";
});
```

3.2 Modal Window:

html

```
<button class="open-modal">Open Modal</button>
<div class="modal" style="display: none;">
    <div class="modal-content">
        <span class="close-modal">&times;</span>
        <p>This is a modal window!</p>
    </div>
</div>
```

javascript

```
const modal = document.querySelector(".modal");
const openModal = document.querySelector(".open-modal");
const closeModal = document.querySelector(".close-modal");

openModal.addEventListener("click", () => {
    modal.style.display = "block";
});

closeModal.addEventListener("click", () => {
    modal.style.display = "none";
```

```
});
```

3.3 Tabs:

html

```html
<div class="tabs">
   <button data-tab="1">Tab 1</button>
   <button data-tab="2">Tab 2</button>
</div>
<div class="content" id="tab-1">Content for Tab 1</div>
<div class="content" id="tab-2" style="display: none;">Content for Tab 2</div>
```

javascript

```javascript
const buttons = document.querySelectorAll(".tabs button");
const contents = document.querySelectorAll(".content");

buttons.forEach((button) => {
   button.addEventListener("click", () => {
      contents.forEach((content) => (content.style.display = "none"));
      document.querySelector(`#tab-${button.dataset.tab}`).style.display =
         "block";
   });
});
```

4. Adding JavaScript Libraries for Animations and Utilities

JavaScript libraries simplify complex tasks and add advanced features to your projects.

4.1 Animations with GSAP (GreenSock):

html

```html
<div class="box"></div>
<script src="https://cdnjs.cloudflare.com/ajax/libs/gsap/3.12.2/gsap.min.js"></script>
<script>
   gsap.to(".box", { x: 300, duration: 2, backgroundColor: "blue" });
</script>
```

4.2 Utility Library: Lodash

- Lodash simplifies array and object manipulation.
- Example:

   javascript

   ```javascript
   import _ from "lodash";

   const array = [1, 2, 3, 4];
   console.log(_.reverse(array)); // [4, 3, 2, 1]
   ```

5. Real-World Example: Dynamic Theme Toggle
HTML:

html

```
<button id="theme-toggle">Toggle Theme</button>
<div class="content">Theme Example Content</div>
```

CSS:

css

```css
body.light-mode {
    background-color: white;
    color: black;
}

body.dark-mode {
    background-color: black;
    color: white;
}
```

JavaScript:

javascript

```javascript
const toggleButton = document.getElementById("theme-toggle");

toggleButton.addEventListener("click", () => {
    document.body.classList.toggle("dark-mode");
});
```

JavaScript is the backbone of web interactivity, enhancing HTML5 and CSS3 by enabling dynamic behavior, DOM manipulation, and advanced animations. Integrating JavaScript into your projects empowers you to create engaging and user-friendly web experiences. In the next part, we'll dive deeper into advanced techniques for building complete, responsive, and interactive web applications. Let's keep scripting!

Chapter 19: Web Accessibility (A11y) Basics

---

1. Understanding Accessibility Guidelines (WCAG)

Accessibility ensures that websites are usable by people with disabilities, including those who rely on assistive technologies. The Web Content Accessibility Guidelines (WCAG) provide a framework for creating accessible content.

1.1 What Is WCAG?

- **Developed by:** W3C (World Wide Web Consortium).
- **Principles:** Websites should be:
    - **Perceivable:** Information must be presented in ways users can perceive.
    - **Operable:** Interfaces must be usable by all (e.g., keyboard navigation).
    - **Understandable:** Content should be clear and predictable.
    - **Robust:** Compatible with assistive technologies.

WCAG Levels:

- **A:** Minimum accessibility standards.

- **AA:** Acceptable accessibility for most users (preferred standard).

- **AAA:** High-level accessibility (hard to achieve for all content).

1.2 Common WCAG Criteria:

- **Text Alternatives:** Provide alt text for images (<img alt="description">).

- **Keyboard Accessibility:** Ensure all functionality is accessible via keyboard.

- **Color Contrast:** Maintain a minimum contrast ratio (4.5:1 for text).

- **Resizable Text:** Allow users to resize text up to 200% without losing functionality.

2. *ARIA Roles and Attributes*

ARIA (Accessible Rich Internet Applications) roles and attributes bridge the gap for dynamic content and assistive technologies.

2.1 What Is ARIA?

- ARIA provides additional context to HTML elements, making them accessible to screen readers.

2.2 Common ARIA Roles:

- **role="button"**: Makes an element behave like a button.

  html

  ```
  <div role="button" tabindex="0" onclick="alert('Clicked!')">Click Me</div>
  ```

- **role="navigation"**: Marks a section as a navigation landmark.

  html

  ```
  <nav role="navigation">Menu</nav>
  ```

2.3 Common ARIA Attributes:

- **aria-label:** Provides a descriptive label.

  html

  ```
  <button aria-label="Close menu">X</button>
  ```

- **aria-hidden:** Hides elements from screen readers.

html

```
<div aria-hidden="true">Decorative Icon</div>
```

- **aria-expanded:** Indicates the expanded or collapsed state of an element.

html

```
<button aria-expanded="false">Toggle</button>
```

3. Designing for Keyboard Navigation and Screen Readers

3.1 Keyboard Navigation:

- Ensure all interactive elements are reachable using the Tab key.
- Use tabindex to control focus order:
  - tabindex="0": Adds the element to the natural tab order.
  - tabindex="-1": Removes the element from the tab order.

Example:

html

```
<a href="#main-content" tabindex="0">Skip to Main Content</a>
```

3.2 Screen Reader Support:

- Use semantic HTML:
  o `<header>`, `<main>`, `<footer>`, `<nav>`, etc.
- Avoid using `<div>` or `<span>` for structural elements unless ARIA roles are added.

Example: Accessible Form:

html

```html
<form>
    <label for="email">Email Address</label>
    <input type="email" id="email" name="email" aria-required="true">
</form>
```

3.3 Focus Management:

- Manage focus dynamically for modals and other UI components.

javascript

```javascript
document.querySelector('.modal').focus();
```

---

4. Tools for Testing Accessibility

Several tools and browser extensions can help identify and fix accessibility issues.

4.1 Automated Testing Tools:

- **Lighthouse:** A built-in tool in Chrome DevTools that audits accessibility.

plaintext

Chrome > DevTools > Lighthouse > Generate Report

- **axe Accessibility Checker:** A browser extension for real-time accessibility testing.

4.2 Color Contrast Checkers:

- **WebAIM Contrast Checker:** Evaluate text contrast against background colors.

4.3 Screen Readers:

- **NVDA (Windows):** Free screen reader for testing.
- **VoiceOver (macOS):** Built-in screen reader.

4.4 Browser Developer Tools:

- Use the Accessibility tab in Chrome DevTools to inspect ARIA roles and labels.

plaintext

Chrome > DevTools > Elements > Accessibility

Web accessibility is a crucial component of modern web development, ensuring that websites are inclusive and usable for all users. By adhering to WCAG guidelines, leveraging ARIA roles, and designing with keyboard navigation and screen readers in mind, developers can create accessible experiences. In the next chapter, we'll delve into performance optimization techniques to ensure fast, efficient websites. Let's keep building!

Chapter 20: Optimizing Performance

1. Minimizing and Combining CSS and JavaScript Files

Large or unoptimized CSS and JavaScript files can slow down page loading. Minimization and combination improve performance.

1.1 Minimizing Files:

- Removes unnecessary spaces, comments, and characters without changing functionality.
- Tools for minification:
    - **CSS:** CSSNano
    - **JavaScript:** UglifyJS

Example: Original CSS:

css

```
body {
    font-size: 16px;
    margin: 0;
}
```

Minimized CSS:

css

```
body{font-size:16px;margin:0;}
```

1.2 Combining Files:

- Combine multiple CSS or JavaScript files into one to reduce HTTP requests.
- Tools for bundling:
  - **Webpack**
  - **Parcel**

Example: Before Combining:

html

```
<link rel="stylesheet" href="header.css">
<link rel="stylesheet" href="footer.css">
```

After Combining:

html

```
<link rel="stylesheet" href="styles.min.css">
```

---

2. Using Responsive Images and Lazy Loading

Images often account for the largest portion of a webpage's size. Optimizing their use can drastically improve performance.

2.1 Responsive Images:

- Use the <picture> element or the srcset attribute to serve images of different sizes based on the viewport.

Example:

html

```
<picture>
    <source srcset="image-large.jpg" media="(min-width: 1024px)">
    <source srcset="image-medium.jpg" media="(min-width: 768px)">
    <img src="image-small.jpg" alt="Example Image">
</picture>
```

2.2 Lazy Loading:

- Delays loading images or videos until they are visible in the viewport.
- Add the loading="lazy" attribute to images.
- Example:

  html

  ```
  <img src="image.jpg" alt="Lazy Loaded Image" loading="lazy">
  ```

- JavaScript Implementation:

  javascript

```javascript
const images = document.querySelectorAll('img[data-src]');
const loadImage = (img) => {
  img.src = img.dataset.src;
};

const observer = new IntersectionObserver((entries, observer) => {
  entries.forEach((entry) => {
    if (entry.isIntersecting) {
      loadImage(entry.target);
      observer.unobserve(entry.target);
    }
  });
});

images.forEach((img) => observer.observe(img));
```

3. Leveraging Browser Caching and Content Delivery Networks (CDNs)

3.1 Browser Caching:

- Instruct browsers to store static resources (CSS, JavaScript, images) locally for future use.
- Use cache-control headers in your server configuration.

plaintext

Cache-Control: max-age=31536000

- Example in Apache:

plaintext

```
<FilesMatch "\.(html|css|js|jpg|png)$">
    Header set Cache-Control "max-age=31536000, public"
</FilesMatch>
```

3.2 Content Delivery Networks (CDNs):

- CDNs store copies of your files on servers worldwide, delivering them from the closest location to the user.
- Popular CDNs:
  - **Cloudflare**
  - **Amazon CloudFront**
  - **Google Cloud CDN**

Example: Replace:

html

```
<script src="/assets/js/script.js"></script>
```

With:

html

```
<script src="https://cdn.example.com/assets/js/script.js"></script>
```

4. Tools for Testing Performance

Regularly testing and optimizing performance ensures your website remains fast and user-friendly.

4.1 Lighthouse (Built into Chrome):

- Provides insights on performance, accessibility, SEO, and more.
- Steps:
    1. Open Chrome DevTools (Ctrl+Shift+I or Cmd+Option+I).
    2. Navigate to the **Lighthouse** tab.
    3. Click **Generate Report**.

4.2 GTmetrix:

- A web-based tool for in-depth performance analysis.
- Features:
    o Provides PageSpeed and YSlow scores.
    o Highlights areas for improvement, such as image optimization or reducing redirects.

Website: GTmetrix

4.3 WebPageTest:

- Offers detailed performance insights, including time-to-first-byte (TTFB) and visual load progression.
- Website: WebPageTest

4.4 Core Web Vitals Report:

- Measures key performance metrics:
  - **Largest Contentful Paint (LCP):** Measures loading performance.
  - **First Input Delay (FID):** Measures interactivity.
  - **Cumulative Layout Shift (CLS):** Measures visual stability.

5. *Real-World Example: Optimizing a Web Page*
Before Optimization:

- Uncompressed images.
- Multiple CSS and JavaScript files.
- No caching or lazy loading.

After Optimization:

1. Combine and minify CSS and JavaScript:

   o Use tools like Webpack to bundle files.

2. Optimize images:

   o Use responsive images and lazy loading.

3. Enable caching:

   o Configure the server for cache-control headers.

4. Use a CDN:

   o Serve static files via Cloudflare.

Result: Reduced page load time, fewer HTTP requests, and improved performance scores.

Optimizing performance is essential for a seamless user experience. By minimizing files, using responsive images, leveraging browser caching, and testing regularly with tools like Lighthouse and GTmetrix, you can ensure your website is fast, efficient, and user-friendly. In the next chapter, we'll explore best practices for deploying your optimized website to production. Let's continue improving!

Chapter 21: Cross-Browser Compatibility

1. Understanding Differences Between Browsers

Different browsers interpret web standards slightly differently, resulting in inconsistencies in rendering and functionality. Ensuring compatibility across browsers is essential for a seamless user experience.

1.1 Key Challenges:

- **Rendering Engines:** Each browser uses a unique rendering engine.
    - **Chrome/Edge:** Blink.
    - **Firefox:** Gecko.
    - **Safari:** WebKit.
- **CSS and JavaScript Variations:** Some modern features may not be supported universally.
- **Vendor Prefixes:** Older CSS features require prefixes like -webkit-, -moz-, and -ms-.

1.2 Examples of Browser Differences:

- **CSS Grid:** Some older versions of browsers support Grid with prefixed syntax.

css

```
display: -ms-grid; /* IE11 */
display: grid;    /* Modern browsers */
```

- **JavaScript APIs:** Features like fetch are not supported in older browsers like IE11, requiring polyfills.

---

2. Using CSS Resets and Normalization

Browsers apply their own default styles to HTML elements, which can vary. Using resets or normalization libraries ensures consistency.

2.1 CSS Reset:

- Removes all default browser styles, providing a clean slate.
- Popular reset:

css

```
/* Meyer Reset */
html, body, div, span, applet, object, iframe,
h1, h2, h3, h4, h5, h6, p, blockquote, pre,
a, abbr, acronym, address, big, cite, code,
```

```
del, dfn, em, img, ins, kbd, q, s, samp,
small, strike, strong, sub, sup, tt, var,
b, u, i, center,
dl, dt, dd, ol, ul, li,
fieldset, form, label, legend,
table, caption, tbody, tfoot, thead, tr, th, td,
article, aside, canvas, details, embed,
figure, figcaption, footer, header, hgroup,
menu, nav, output, ruby, section, summary,
time, mark, audio, video {
    margin: 0;
    padding: 0;
    border: 0;
    font-size: 100%;
    font: inherit;
    vertical-align: baseline;
}
```

2.2 CSS Normalization:

- Retains useful default styles and normalizes differences between browsers.

- Popular library: Normalize.css.

- Example:

css

```
html {
    line-height: 1.15; /* Adjust default browser line height */
```

```
}
```

---

3. Writing Fallbacks for Unsupported Features

When using modern CSS or JavaScript features, provide fallbacks to ensure functionality in older browsers.

3.1 CSS Fallbacks:

- Define a simpler property before the advanced one.

css

```css
background: #000; /* Fallback for browsers without gradients */
background: linear-gradient(to right, #000, #fff);
```

CSS Variables Fallback:

- Use a default value if a variable is unsupported.

css

```css
color: var(--primary-color, #000);
```

3.2 JavaScript Fallbacks:

- Use feature detection to check for API support.

javascript

```
if ('fetch' in window) {
    fetch('/api/data').then(response => response.json());
} else {
    // Use XMLHttpRequest for older browsers
    const xhr = new XMLHttpRequest();
    xhr.open('GET', '/api/data', true);
    xhr.onload = () => console.log(JSON.parse(xhr.responseText));
    xhr.send();
}
```

Polyfills:

- Add missing features to older browsers.
- Example: Include the fetch polyfill.

html

```
<script
src="https://cdnjs.cloudflare.com/ajax/libs/fetch/3.6.2/fetch.min.js"></s
cript>
```

3.3 Vendor Prefixes:

- Use tools like Autoprefixer to add prefixes automatically.
- Example:

css

```
.box {
```

```
    display: -webkit-box; /* Older WebKit */
    display: -ms-flexbox; /* IE10 */
    display: flex;      /* Modern browsers */
}
```

4. Testing on Multiple Browsers and Devices

Testing ensures your website functions correctly across different platforms.

4.1 Browser Testing Tools:

- **BrowserStack:** Cloud-based platform for testing on real browsers and devices.
- **CrossBrowserTesting:** Test on hundreds of browser/device combinations.
- **Lambdatest:** A reliable tool for live and automated testing.

4.2 Manual Testing:

- Install multiple browsers on your local machine (e.g., Chrome, Firefox, Safari).
- Test on mobile devices using browser developer tools:
    - **Chrome DevTools:** Toggle device mode.
    - **Firefox DevTools:** Responsive design mode.

4.3 Emulating Browsers with Virtual Machines:

- Use virtual machines to test older browsers like IE11.
- Microsoft provides free VMs for testing: IE Virtual Machines.

4.4 Testing for Accessibility:

- Use screen readers and keyboard navigation to check functionality.

5. Real-World Example: Cross-Browser Styling
HTML:

html

```html
<div class="feature-box">Cross-Browser Box</div>
```

CSS:

css

```css
.feature-box {
    display: -webkit-box; /* Old WebKit */
    display: -ms-flexbox; /* IE10 */
    display: flex;        /* Modern browsers */
    background: #000;     /* Fallback */
```

```
background: linear-gradient(to right, #000, #fff);
padding: 20px;
color: white;
}
```

Cross-browser compatibility ensures a consistent experience for all users, regardless of their browser or device. By understanding browser differences, using resets and normalization, writing fallbacks, and testing thoroughly, you can minimize compatibility issues. In the next chapter, we'll explore the final steps of deploying your optimized, accessible, and compatible website to production. Let's keep building!

Chapter 22: Deploying Your Website

1. Choosing a Hosting Platform

Selecting the right hosting platform is critical for making your website publicly accessible. Hosting platforms differ in cost, features, and ease of deployment.

1.1 Popular Hosting Platforms:

1. **Netlify:**
   - o Ideal for static sites.
   - o Features:
     - Continuous deployment from GitHub/GitLab/Bitbucket.
     - Built-in SSL certificate provisioning.
   - o Deployment steps:

     0. Create a Netlify account.
     1. Link your Git repository.
     2. Configure build settings (e.g., npm run build for React).
     3. Deploy.

2. **GitHub Pages:**

o   Perfect for simple static sites and documentation.

o   Features:

- Free hosting for public repositories.
- Supports Jekyll for static site generation.

o   Deployment steps:

0. Push your files to a GitHub repository.
1. Go to the repository settings and enable GitHub Pages.

3. **Vercel:**

o   Designed for modern JavaScript frameworks (Next.js, Nuxt.js).

o   Features:

- Automatic deployment.
- Edge caching for fast delivery.

4. **Amazon Web Services (AWS):**

o   Ideal for dynamic or enterprise-scale applications.

o   Features:

- Amazon S3 for static sites.
- Elastic Beanstalk or EC2 for dynamic apps.

1.2 Static Sites vs. Dynamic Sites:

- **Static Sites:** Consist of HTML, CSS, and JavaScript. Examples: blogs, portfolios.
- **Dynamic Sites:** Generate content dynamically based on user input or backend data. Examples: e-commerce sites, social networks.

2. Setting Up Your Domain and SSL Certificate

2.1 Registering a Domain:

- Use a domain registrar like:
    - **Namecheap**
    - **Google Domains**
    - **GoDaddy**

Example:

- Register example.com and point it to your hosting platform using DNS settings.

2.2 Linking a Custom Domain to Your Host:

For Netlify:

1. Go to your Netlify site dashboard.

2. Under "Domain Settings," add a custom domain.

3. Update your domain registrar's DNS settings to point to Netlify's servers.

For GitHub Pages:

1. Add a CNAME file in your repository with your custom domain.

2. Update your DNS settings to point to GitHub's IP addresses.

2.3 Adding SSL Certificates:

- SSL certificates ensure secure connections (HTTPS).
- Many platforms provide free SSL certificates:
  - o **Netlify** and **Vercel:** Auto-provision SSL.
  - o **Let's Encrypt:** Free SSL certificates for custom setups.
- Verify SSL installation using tools like SSL Labs.

---

3. Deploying Static Sites vs. Dynamic Sites

3.1 Deploying Static Sites:

- **Process:**

- o Build your site locally (e.g., using a static site generator like Jekyll or Gatsby).
- o Upload files to the host (via Git, FTP, or drag-and-drop).
- Example: Deploying to Netlify

bash

git push origin main

- o Netlify detects changes and deploys the updated site.

3.2 Deploying Dynamic Sites:

- **Process:**
    - o Set up a server (e.g., Node.js, Django).
    - o Deploy backend code to platforms like AWS EC2, Heroku, or DigitalOcean.
- Example: Deploying a Node.js app to Heroku

bash

heroku create
git push heroku main

Database Setup:

- Use managed database services like AWS RDS, Firebase, or MongoDB Atlas for dynamic applications.

---

4. Introduction to Continuous Integration/Deployment (CI/CD)

CI/CD automates the testing, building, and deployment processes, ensuring rapid and reliable delivery of updates.

4.1 What Is CI/CD?

- **Continuous Integration (CI):**
  - Automates the testing and integration of code changes into a shared repository.
- **Continuous Deployment (CD):**
  - Automatically deploys changes to production after passing tests.

4.2 Benefits of CI/CD:

- Faster updates with reduced downtime.
- Ensures consistent builds across environments.
- Early detection of bugs via automated testing.

4.3 Setting Up CI/CD:

- Use platforms like:
    - **GitHub Actions**: Automate workflows directly in GitHub.
    - **CircleCI**: Easy integration with repositories.
    - **GitLab CI/CD**: Built-in for GitLab repositories.

4.4 Example CI/CD Workflow with GitHub Actions:

Step 1: Create a .github/workflows/deploy.yml File

yaml

```
name: CI/CD Pipeline

on:
 push:
  branches:
   - main

jobs:
 build-deploy:
  runs-on: ubuntu-latest

  steps:
  - name: Checkout Code
   uses: actions/checkout@v2
```

```
- name: Install Dependencies
  run: npm install


- name: Build Project
  run: npm run build


- name: Deploy to Netlify
  uses: netlify/actions/deploy@v1
  with:
    NETLIFY_AUTH_TOKEN: ${{ secrets.NETLIFY_AUTH_TOKEN }}
    NETLIFY_SITE_ID: ${{ secrets.NETLIFY_SITE_ID }}
```

Step 2: Add Secrets:

1. Go to the GitHub repository settings.
2. Add NETLIFY_AUTH_TOKEN and NETLIFY_SITE_ID as secrets.

Step 3: Push Changes:

- Committing changes to the main branch triggers the workflow, automating the build and deployment process.

Deploying a website is the final step in bringing your project to life. By choosing the right hosting platform, setting up custom domains and SSL certificates, and leveraging CI/CD pipelines, you can ensure a smooth deployment process. With your website now live and optimized, you're ready to deliver exceptional user experiences. Let's take your web development skills to the next level!

Chapter 23: Building a Portfolio Website

1. Designing a Responsive Portfolio Layout

A portfolio website showcases your skills, projects, and personality to potential employers or clients. It should be visually appealing, easy to navigate, and fully responsive.

1.1 Planning Your Layout:

- **Essential Sections:**
    1. **Header:** Your name/logo, navigation links, and a call-to-action (CTA) button.
    2. **About:** A brief introduction and bio.
    3. **Portfolio/Projects:** Display your work with descriptions and images.
    4. **Contact:** Email, social media links, or a contact form.
    5. **Footer:** Additional links or copyright information.

1.2 HTML Structure:

html

```
<header>
  <nav>
```

```html
      <a href="#about">About</a>
      <a href="#portfolio">Portfolio</a>
      <a href="#contact">Contact</a>
   </nav>
</header>
<section id="about">
   <h1>Your Name</h1>
   <p>A short bio about your skills and experience.</p>
</section>
<section id="portfolio">
   <h2>My Projects</h2>
   <div class="gallery">
      <div class="project">
         <img src="project1.jpg" alt="Project 1">
         <h3>Project Title</h3>
         <p>Brief description of the project.</p>
      </div>
   </div>
</section>
<section id="contact">
   <h2>Contact Me</h2>
   <form>
      <input type="email" placeholder="Your Email">
      <textarea placeholder="Your Message"></textarea>
      <button type="submit">Send</button>
   </form>
</section>
<footer>
   <p>© 2024 Your Name</p>
</footer>
```

1.3 Responsive CSS:

- Use a mobile-first approach with media queries for larger screens.

css

```css
body {
    font-family: Arial, sans-serif;
    margin: 0;
    padding: 0;
}

header nav {
    display: flex;
    justify-content: center;
    gap: 20px;
}

.gallery {
    display: grid;
    grid-template-columns: repeat(auto-fit, minmax(200px, 1fr));
    gap: 20px;
}

@media (min-width: 768px) {
    header nav {
        justify-content: flex-end;
```

```
  }

  .gallery {
    grid-template-columns: repeat(3, 1fr);
  }
}
```

2. Adding Interactive Elements (Image Galleries, Animations)

Interactive elements make your portfolio engaging and professional.

2.1 Image Galleries:

- Use a grid layout for your projects with hover effects.

css

```css
.project img {
  transition: transform 0.3s ease;
}

.project:hover img {
  transform: scale(1.1);
}
```

Adding a Lightbox Effect:

- Use JavaScript for a lightbox to display images in full screen.

javascript

```javascript
const images = document.querySelectorAll(".project img");
images.forEach((img) => {
  img.addEventListener("click", () => {
    const lightbox = document.createElement("div");
    lightbox.classList.add("lightbox");
    const imgClone = img.cloneNode();
    lightbox.appendChild(imgClone);
    document.body.appendChild(lightbox);

    lightbox.addEventListener("click", () => {
      document.body.removeChild(lightbox);
    });
  });
});
```

2.2 Animations:

- Use CSS animations for smooth transitions.

css

```css
@keyframes fadeIn {
  from {
    opacity: 0;
  }
  to {
    opacity: 1;
  }
}
```

```
.project {
    animation: fadeIn 0.5s ease-in-out;
}
```

3. Optimizing for SEO and Performance

3.1 SEO Best Practices:

- Add meta tags:

  html

  ```html
  <head>
      <meta name="description" content="Portfolio website showcasing projects and skills">
      <meta name="keywords" content="portfolio, web development, projects">
  </head>
  ```

- Use descriptive alt text for images.
- Add a sitemap and robots.txt file.

3.2 Performance Optimization:

- Compress images with tools like TinyPNG.
- Minify CSS and JavaScript.

215

- Implement lazy loading for images:

html

```
<img src="placeholder.jpg" data-src="actual-image.jpg" loading="lazy"
alt="Project Image">
```

4. Deploying the Portfolio Online

4.1 Choosing a Hosting Platform:

- **Netlify:** Free and easy deployment for static sites.
- **GitHub Pages:** Ideal for small, static portfolios.

4.2 Deploying to GitHub Pages:

1. Push your portfolio files to a GitHub repository.
2. Go to **Settings > Pages** and select the branch to deploy.
3. Access your site at https://yourusername.github.io/your-repo-name.

4.3 Deploying to Netlify:

1. Create a Netlify account and link your GitHub repository.
2. Configure build settings if necessary (e.g., npm run build for React).

3. Deploy and access your portfolio via the Netlify-provided domain or a custom domain.

Building a portfolio website allows you to showcase your skills and projects professionally. By designing a responsive layout, adding interactive elements, optimizing for SEO and performance, and deploying your site online, you can create a portfolio that impresses potential employers and clients. In the next chapter, we'll build a more advanced real-world project: a blog platform using HTML5, CSS3, and JavaScript. Let's keep creating!

Chapter 24: Creating a Blog Layout

---

1. Structuring a Blog Homepage and Individual Posts

A blog layout should be well-organized, visually appealing, and user-friendly: It typically includes a homepage displaying multiple posts and individual pages for each post.

1.1 Blog Homepage Structure:

- **Essential Elements:**
    1. **Header:** Blog title, navigation links, and search bar.
    2. **Featured Posts Section:** Highlight recent or popular posts.
    3. **Post Listings:** A list of posts with titles, excerpts, and "Read More" links.

HTML Example:

html

```
<header>
  <h1>My Blog</h1>
  <nav>
    <a href="#">Home</a>
    <a href="#about">About</a>
```

```
      <a href="#contact">Contact</a>
   </nav>
</header>
<main>
   <section class="featured-posts">
      <h2>Featured Posts</h2>
      <div class="post">
         <h3>Post Title</h3>
         <p>Post excerpt goes here...</p>
         <a href="post.html">Read More</a>
      </div>
   </section>
   <section class="post-list">
      <h2>Latest Posts</h2>
      <div class="post">
         <h3>Post Title</h3>
         <p>Post excerpt goes here...</p>
         <a href="post.html">Read More</a>
      </div>
   </section>
</main>
<footer>
   <p>© 2024 My Blog</p>
</footer>
```

1.2 Individual Post Page Structure:

- **Essential Elements:**

  1. **Post Header:** Title, author, date, and categories.

2. **Post Content:** Full blog post content, including images and text.

3. **Comments Section:** Display user comments and a form to add new comments.

HTML Example:

html

```
<article>
  <header>
    <h1>Post Title</h1>
    <p>By <span>Author Name</span> on <time datetime="2024-12-22">December 22, 2024</time></p>
  </header>
  <section>
    <p>Full blog post content goes here...</p>
  </section>
</article>
<section class="comments">
  <h2>Comments</h2>
  <div class="comment">
    <p><strong>User:</strong> This is a great post!</p>
  </div>
</section>
```

2. Using CSS Grid and Flexbox for Layout

CSS Grid and Flexbox are ideal for creating flexible, responsive blog layouts.

2.1 Blog Homepage Layout:

- Use Grid for the overall structure and Flexbox for individual post cards.

CSS Example:

```css
css

main {
    display: grid;
    grid-template-columns: 1fr;
    gap: 20px;
    padding: 20px;
}

.featured-posts, .post-list {
    display: grid;
    grid-template-columns: repeat(auto-fit, minmax(200px, 1fr));
    gap: 20px;
}

.post {
    display: flex;
    flex-direction: column;
    padding: 20px;
    border: 1px solid #ccc;
    border-radius: 5px;
    background-color: #f9f9f9;
```

```
}
```

2.2 Individual Post Layout:

- Use a Grid layout to separate the content and sidebar (optional).

CSS Example:

css

```css
article {
    display: grid;
    grid-template-columns: 3fr 1fr;
    gap: 20px;
    padding: 20px;
}

article section {
    grid-column: 1;
}

aside {
    grid-column: 2;
    border: 1px solid #ccc;
    padding: 20px;
}
```

---

3. Adding a Comments Section with Forms

Interactive comments sections engage readers and add value to your blog.

HTML Example:

html

```
<section class="comments">
  <h2>Comments</h2>
  <div class="comment">
    <p><strong>Jane Doe:</strong> Great post!</p>
  </div>
  <form>
    <label for="name">Name:</label>
    <input type="text" id="name" placeholder="Your Name" required>

    <label for="comment">Comment:</label>
    <textarea id="comment" placeholder="Your Comment" required></textarea>

    <button type="submit">Submit</button>
  </form>
</section>
```

CSS for Styling Comments Section:

css

```
.comments {
  margin-top: 20px;
```

```css
    padding: 20px;
    border-top: 1px solid #ccc;
}


.comment {
    margin-bottom: 10px;
    padding: 10px;
    background-color: #f5f5f5;
    border-radius: 5px;
}


form {
    display: flex;
    flex-direction: column;
    gap: 10px;
}


form input, form textarea {
    padding: 10px;
    border: 1px solid #ccc;
    border-radius: 5px;
}


form button {
    padding: 10px;
    background-color: #3498db;
    color: white;
    border: none;
    border-radius: 5px;
    cursor: pointer;
```

}

JavaScript for Form Submission:

javascript

```
document.querySelector('form').addEventListener('submit', (e) => {
  e.preventDefault();
  const name = document.getElementById('name').value;
  const comment = document.getElementById('comment').value;

  const commentSection = document.querySelector('.comments');
  const newComment = document.createElement('div');
  newComment.classList.add('comment');
  newComment.innerHTML        =        `<p><strong>${name}:</strong>
${comment}</p>`;
  commentSection.appendChild(newComment);

  document.getElementById('name').value = '';
  document.getElementById('comment').value = '';
});
```

4. Making the Blog Mobile-Friendly

Mobile responsiveness is critical for ensuring a positive user experience across devices.

Mobile-Friendly CSS:

- Use media queries to adjust layouts for smaller screens.

css

```css
@media (max-width: 768px) {
  main {
    grid-template-columns: 1fr;
  }

  article {
    grid-template-columns: 1fr;
  }

  .post {
    flex-direction: column;
  }
}
```

Creating a blog layout involves structuring a homepage, designing individual post pages, and adding interactive features like comments sections. By leveraging CSS Grid, Flexbox, and responsive design principles, you can ensure your blog is visually appealing and user-friendly across devices. In the next chapter, we'll create a complete e-commerce website to showcase advanced web development techniques. Let's keep coding!

Chapter 25: Designing an E-Commerce Landing Page

1. Key Elements of an E-Commerce Page

An effective e-commerce landing page should be visually appealing, intuitive, and functional. Here are the core elements:

1.1 Essential Components:

1. **Header:**
   - Includes a logo, navigation links (e.g., Home, Shop, About, Contact), and a search bar.
   - Example:

   html

   ```
   <header>
     <h1>ShopLogo</h1>
     <nav>
       <a href="#">Home</a>
       <a href="#">Shop</a>
       <a href="#">Contact</a>
     </nav>
     <input type="text" placeholder="Search products">
     <div class="cart-icon">◻</div>
   ```

```
</header>
```

2. Product Grid:

- o Displays products with an image, name, price, and "Add to Cart" button.
- o Example:

html

```
<section class="product-grid">
  <div class="product">
    <img src="product1.jpg" alt="Product 1">
    <h2>Product 1</h2>
    <p>$20.00</p>
    <button>Add to Cart</button>
  </div>
</section>
```

3. Filters and Sorting:

- o Allow users to filter by categories, price range, or ratings.
- o Example:

html

```
<aside class="filters">
  <h3>Filters</h3>
  <label><input type="checkbox"> Category 1</label>
  <label><input type="checkbox"> Category 2</label>
```

```
<input type="range" min="0" max="100" value="50">
</aside>
```

4. **Cart Section:**

   o Displays selected products and total price.

   o Example:

   html

```
<section class="cart">
  <h2>Shopping Cart</h2>
  <div class="cart-item">
    <p>Product 1</p>
    <p>$20.00</p>
  </div>
  <button>Checkout</button>
</section>
```

2. Responsive Design for Multiple Devices

Responsive design ensures your e-commerce page adapts seamlessly to different screen sizes.

2.1 Desktop Layout:

- Use CSS Grid for the overall structure and Flexbox for individual components.

css

```css
.product-grid {
   display: grid;
   grid-template-columns: repeat(4, 1fr);
   gap: 20px;
}

.product {
   display: flex;
   flex-direction: column;
   align-items: center;
}
```

2.2 Mobile Layout:

- Adjust the grid to display fewer products in a row.

css

```css
@media (max-width: 768px) {
   .product-grid {
      grid-template-columns: repeat(2, 1fr);
   }
}

@media (max-width: 480px) {
   .product-grid {
      grid-template-columns: 1fr;
   }
}
```

}

2.3 Navigation for Mobile:

- Use a hamburger menu for compact navigation.

html

```html
<div class="hamburger-menu">≡</div>
<nav class="mobile-nav">
   <a href="#">Home</a>
   <a href="#">Shop</a>
   <a href="#">Contact</a>
</nav>
```

CSS:

css

```css
.mobile-nav {
   display: none;
   flex-direction: column;
}

.hamburger-menu {
   display: block;
   cursor: pointer;
}

.hamburger-menu:hover + .mobile-nav {
   display: flex;
```

```
}
```

---

3. Accessibility Considerations for Forms and Navigation

Accessibility ensures all users, including those with disabilities, can interact with your e-commerce page.

3.1 Accessible Forms:

- Use label elements to associate text with input fields.
- Example:

html

```
<label for="search">Search Products</label>
<input id="search" type="text" placeholder="Search products">
```

3.2 Keyboard Navigation:

- Ensure all interactive elements (buttons, links, inputs) are focusable using tabindex.

html

```
<button tabindex="0">Add to Cart</button>
```

3.3 ARIA Roles and Attributes:

- Provide additional context for assistive technologies.
  - Example: Role for a navigation bar.

html

```
<nav role="navigation">
  <a href="#">Home</a>
  <a href="#">Shop</a>
</nav>
```

3.4 Color Contrast:

- Ensure text contrasts with its background for readability.
  - o Example:

css

```
body {
  color: #000;
  background-color: #fff;
}
```

---

4. Deploying the E-Commerce Page for Testing

4.1 Choose a Hosting Platform:

- **Netlify** or **Vercel** for static pages.
- **Heroku** or **AWS** for dynamic e-commerce platforms.

4.2 Deployment Steps:

1. Push your code to a Git repository (e.g., GitHub, GitLab).

2. Link the repository to a hosting service (e.g., Netlify or Vercel).

3. Configure build settings (e.g., npm run build for React projects).

4. Deploy and access the page via the hosting platform's URL.

4.3 Testing the Deployed Page:

- Use tools like **BrowserStack** or **Lighthouse** to test cross-device functionality.
- Validate accessibility with tools like **axe Accessibility Checker** or **WAVE**.

Designing an e-commerce landing page requires a combination of functionality, accessibility, and responsive design. By incorporating essential elements like product grids, filters, and a cart section while ensuring mobile compatibility and accessibility, you can create an intuitive and user-friendly shopping experience. Deploy your project to test its performance and usability in real-world scenarios. This chapter concludes your journey in designing professional web projects—apply these techniques to build amazing websites!

www.ingramcontent.com/pod-product-compliance
Lightning Source LLC
La Vergne TN
LVHW051321050326
832903LV00031B/3302